PUTTING MYSELF IN THE PICTURE

PUTTING MYSELF IN THE PICTURE

A POLITICAL, PERSONAL AND PHOTOGRAPHIC AUTOBIOGRAPHY

JO SPENCE

Art Series Editor: Frances Borzello

Camden Press

Published in 1986 by
Camden Press Ltd
43 Camden Passage, London N1 8EB, England

Text and photographs © Jo Spence 1986

Designed by Anne Braybon

Set in Baskerville 11/12 pt
by Inforum Ltd, Portsmouth
and printed and bound by
Bath Press, Avon

British Library CIP Data

Spence, Jo
Putting myself in the picture, a political, personal
and photographic autobiography
1. Spence, Jo
2. Photographers—England—Biography
I. Title
770′.92′4   TR140.56/

ISBN 0–948491–14–0–

This book is dedicated to my mother and father,
my brother Michael,
my nieces Lisa and Jo, to Terry,
to my recently adopted sisters Margaret Joan and Sophie,
and to David who is beyond description.

Thank you

ACKNOWLEDGMENTS

In my life I have met some quite extraordinary people. Many of them I loved and shared my life with. Others taught me, or worked with me. My thanks to all of them.

Additionally, in the past four years in a journey towards a search for better health I met some even more extraordinary folk who were involved in the holistic health movement. My particular thanks to Yana Stajno and David Lurie for their unstinting love and care in my health programme, and to Peter Clark who taught me to co-counsel and that one cuddle is worth a thousand words.

Thanks to Frankie Borzello who has been a very nurturing editor, to Anne Braybon who has designed order out of chaos and to Terry Dennett for all the work he put into helping this book to emerge from the original exhibition.

Especial thanks to David Roberts for his daily loving sustenance and editorial help whilst we did the cooking together.

I am grateful to *Ten. 8* for permission to reproduce 'Public Image Private Functions'; *City Limits* for 'Confronting Cancer'; *Screen* for 'Remodelling Photo History'; Liz Heron for 'Who's Still Holding the Camera?'; W.W. Norton and Company for the poem by Adrienne Rich from *On Lies, Secrets and Silence*; and to Methuen, London, for the quotation from Bertolt Brecht's 'Questions From a Worker Who Reads', translated by Michael Hamburger.

CONTENTS

In speaking of lies,
we come inevitably,
to the subject of truth.
There is nothing simple
or easy about this idea.
There is no 'the truth!'
'a truth' —
truth is not one thing
or even a system.
It is an increasing
complexity.
The pattern of the carpet
is the surface.
When we look closely
or when we become weavers,
we learn of the tiny multiple threads
unseen in the overall
pattern, the knots on the
underside of the carpet.

Adrienne Rich

From a photo therapy session on the end of my anal phase.

INTRODUCTION

This book developed out of an exhibition of my involvement with photography from 1950 up to the present time. This *Review of Work* was commissioned by the Cambridge Darkroom in March 1985 and has since been on a national tour of the UK.

Many who found the exhibition stimulating nonetheless complained that there was too much work to do standing in a gallery reading my longwinded texts and trying to make sense of so wide a range of approaches to photography. In time I came to realize that a book format might be more accessible. Something that could be studied and enjoyed at leisure, rather than worried over and hurried through.

The original show took the form of several discrete sections, each covering a part of my life, weaving between the personal, the political and the autobiographical, and I have followed this form in the book. While the book is arranged chronologically, the journey was never straightforward and the separate sections should not be seen as developments in any conventional way.

As an account of work grounded in my involvement with a variety of cultural debates, it is in no way unproblematically about me as 'author', but is rather an indication of how my thought processes worked, changed and appeared within my photographic work. In mapping out a series of explanations, arguments and descriptions, I endeavour to offer an account of the way in which one photographer has continually changed. I want this to stand in contradiction to the usual 'history of photography' approach, which carefully arranges photographers in schools and genres, assumes that mostly we work alone, and perpetuates various myths about creativity, rather than acknowledging that we are positioned within a cultural and economic network of relationships. Although some photographers assume a practice and then stay rigidly, and quite happily, within it and others shift their practice gradually across time, there are many like myself who inhabit several different practices in the same period.

What follows then is one account of my journey through life and photography, and how they fed into and off each other. It is not for me to explain what the work is 'about', but I hope it will be used as a jumping-off point for discussion and argument. I hope also that it will encourage those who own cameras but hardly ever use

1938, a crucial year in my life. War broke out, my brother Michael was born, I started school, and I was evacuated. On a visit from Grandpa Bill, the new baby is shown off.

them, to see that the most simple pictures can be used to start off a chain of ideas, or to contradict notions of what we think we know. The camera is an extremely undervalued tool whose uses have hardly begun.

This book is only the beginning of a map. In that I hope you, my readers, share at least some common cultural assumptions with me, I hope it will enable you to ask similar questions about your own particular history.

WHITE COLLAR OFFICE WORKER 1949 TO 1964

After leaving school at thirteen (having failed my exams for entry to 'the Tech') I was put through private secretarial college for two years by my parents, both of whom worked in factories and wanted 'something better' for me. At fifteen I started my first job at the Fellowship for Freedom in Medicine, a right-wing body of doctors who had organized themselves in opposition to the new National Health Service. Here I was the office girl. From 1951 to 1962 I worked as shorthand typist/book-keeper/secretary for a small commercial photographers in Finchley Road, London, called Photo Coverage. They took photos for advertising agencies, architects, public relations companies, newspapers, and also for a broad range of large and small commercial enterprises. They also had a retail outlet which sold cameras and took in developing and printing and I was sent on a training course at Kodak so that I could be a 'useful' shop assistant. Through this contact with the public, they covered weddings and barmitzvahs and did family groups and child photography. During my eleven years there I gradually became interested in photography as I helped out in almost every area. Here I bought my first professional camera and got my own small commissions to do weddings and portraiture for friends and neighbours. I received no formal training but picked everything up by watching others carry out their everyday photographic practice. Nothing was ever viewed critically, no job was ever turned down. Technique was everything. Was it sharp? In the middle of the frame? Well lit and exposed? If a client was not happy with the work, it had to be re-shot, or not charged for. Time was money.

In those days photographic companies often ran apprenticeship schemes which involved signing indentures for three or four years training on the job plus the privilege of attending trade school one day a week. After years of arranging for others to attend college I conceived the idea that I also might go. This I managed to arrange in 1962. I lasted only about half a term and was very disruptive, always pointing out that 'It's not done like that in a real commercial studio'. I also fell in love and felt this to be a more important priority on my time. During this period I was much influenced by a close woman friend, Lizette Elles, a portrait photographer. Finally I broke away from secretarial work and

became a girl friday for a Fleet Street-turned-advertising photographer, working for him on a part-time basis. Later I went to work for a well-known Canadian advertising photographer, Walter Curtin, as his assistant, secretary and printer. For this I was paid £15 a week. During these periods I learned a lot about how to handle clients, visualize work from an advertising brief, arrange sets and props, book models, find locations and set up lighting. In fact do everything except take the actual shot.

This move from secretarial to photographic worker far exceeded my class expectations and was viewed by me as very exciting and challenging. However, I never saw in myself the potential to become what my various bosses were. I imagined that, at most, I could be a portrait photographer like my friend Lizette, but didn't have the faintest idea how to go about achieving such an ambition. Anyway, I was nearing thirty and already perceived myself to be on the shelf and marriage beckoned.

None of this early work, to which I contributed but could not claim 'authorship', is available for me to use. It never belonged to me, nor did I have any rights over it as a waged labourer.

A photograph taken by Stephen Taffler of Photo Coverage, London, for the careers editor of the magazine My Home. *It shows the photography department at the Regent Street Polytechnic in 1952. I assisted him on this occasion as caption writer.*

Whilst working as a shorthand typist, I often accompanied photographers on jobs and acted as their caption writer. This meant that immediately after a group of people had been photographed (usually for a hairdressing or catering industry trade magazine), I would step forward, notebook and pencil in hand, and ask them for their full names and relevant details. I'd also encourage them to purchase copies of the photograph. On these occasions I would be dressed in a black taffeta skirt and white blouse, with black suede ballerina slippers. In this way I would be 'well dressed' and 'discreet', neither vying with those present in a social capacity, nor standing out by dressing inappropriately. I was therefore invisible . . . except that there were running battles between me and the editor of *Hairdressers' Journal* over the untidiness of my hair.

One of our regular clients in those days was a women's magazine called *My Home*, whose careers editor was named Bethea Creese. She was a delightful old soul, feminist to the core, and always thinking up assignments for us in far flung parts of the British Isles. On one occasion we had to visit the photography department of the Regent Street Polytechnic to document women learning photography. On this occasion I took the captions. It never crossed my mind that I could ever step out of my (as I saw it then) fixed class position and become a student, and it was not until I was in my mid-forties that I found the courage to attend that same college as a full time student (now called the Polytechnic of Central London), from which I emerged with a first-class honours degree.

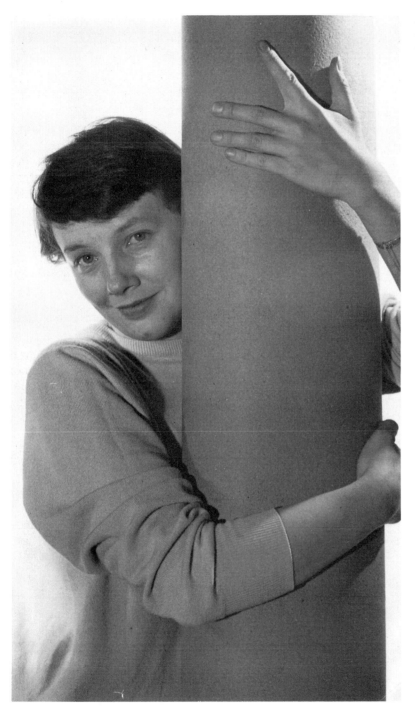

A session in the studio after work. I'm the model, wanting to be a cover girl.

*C*AMERA CLUB DAYS *EARLY 1960s*

During the time I worked as a secretary and dreamed of becoming a photographer (a total fantasy at that point) I joined the Hampstead Camera Club. Here we had 'slide battles': great experts came to judge our monthly print competitions, and men clustered in corners talking about hypo and developers. Periodically we engaged a nude model and set up our lights whilst she stripped off. We then spent the next session discussing our individual (but oh so similar) results.

I drew from the repertoire of image-making which seemed to be appropriate to belonging to such a club, and settled on the photography of children. My speciality was the spontaneous cute shot ('children will be children, you know').

I thoroughly enjoyed the meetings and outings and through the club got involved with a local photographer, Sydney Weaver, who came to give a talk to us about portraiture. By this time several of my boyfriends were photographers and I was always being photographed, usually to use up the end of a film from a job so as not to waste any unused frames.

*Pictures of the children of
friends, neighbours and
relatives were my staple
subject at the local camera
club. I looked for
spontaneity and naughtiness
in boys, tranquillity and
prettiness in girls.*

F ARM SECRETARY
1965

During my short marriage I worked for a while as a farm secretary. This meant that we moved to Hampshire to live on the estate of an aristocratic owner, alongside other employees, and I was allocated a 'free' cottage next door to the head gardener. Although the wages were low, we lived like lords!

As I never had enough work to keep me fully occupied, I mentioned to my employer that I had previously been a photographer. He asked me if I would like to make an inventory of his land and properties with my camera. Some of the photographs seen here were produced for this and gave a clear indication to me (with hindsight) that I treated the farmworkers, literally, as being the property of their Lord and Master. It is interesting for me to look now at these photographs and see the shifts across from straight 'record' photography into 'pictorial' photography. This difference reflected the reality to some degree, the parts of the farm inhabited by the owners being very pictorial, whilst the farm labourers' cottages were much more like urban terraced housing built for industrial workers at the turn of the century.

As well as the pictures seen here I produced a private family album of colour photographs for the family I worked for. These were mostly pictures of their lavish grounds and gardens and of themselves at play. I did not keep the negatives.

During this period I became very conscious of my relative class position (low status), and experienced first hand the power and property relations of people belonging to the ruling classes. I daily observed the strict hierarchy of command on the farm and amongst the house servants. As the 'invisible' secretary, I was also able to overhear how government information was circulated and support for different matters mobilized by apparently benign patriarchs masquerading under the guise of country gentlemen.

By my standards Brockwood Park was magnificent, although as country houses and grounds go it was in the minor league.

The cook at work in the kitchens.

*One family's pleasure is
another's work.*

*The farmworkers' point of
view.*

The house owners' point of view.

*H*IGH STREET PHOTOGRAPHER
1967 TO 1974

In 1967, after a failed marriage and then a failed 'elopement' to Ireland, ending in physical illness and nervous breakdown, I found myself back in Hampstead. I looked in on old friend, Sydney Weaver, only to find that he was on the point of giving up his studio and moving to Germany. After several meetings at which we discussed his chronic depression, he tentatively suggested that I might be a suitable person to take over his portrait studio.

As I was fairly highly drugged on anti-depressants at the time it seemed a good idea to me. Borrowing £300 from my parents for the first quarter's rent and for the fixtures and fittings (a black velvet curtain, a spotlight, a drymounter and an old enlarger), I went into business. I borrowed some suitable specimen portraits from Lizette to put in the showcase in the mews outside, and waited. After a few months I invited Michael Balfre, a commercial photographer with whom I had worked at Photo Coverage, to join me. Thus we ran two different businesses under the same roof and kept our expenses to a minimum.

I had previously only done portraiture out of doors, (making a virtue out of the fact that I had no studio, telling clients that their pictures would look 'more natural'). Now I learned everything on the job and all my early clients were guinea pigs while I improved my technique. Initially it merely consisted of getting things sharp, centered, and well exposed. Later as I began to evolve a 'personal' style I took more risks. Contrary to my belief that I was inventing my technique, I realize with hindsight that my work was totally of its period and influenced by the dominant trends in portrait photography. I had already internalized various ways of encoding photographs from watching others at work, from reading magazines and from the cinema.

As I became more proficient, literally by the process of trial and error and listening to what people said when they looked through their proofs, I started to evolve particular styles of lighting and techniques for handling clients and putting them at their ease.

I began to make a good name as an actors' photographer who produced pictures which helped get people work. My speciality was the production of portfolios for professional use, and in the evolution of this work I learned the art of visual stereotyping.

joanna
spence

photography

6 rosslyn mews rosslyn hill london nw3 01-794 3747

Sometimes actors would try out new 'selves' for the camera, and I would try to interpret their needs in the light of what they presented to me, what they said, and the parts they were trying to get.

This practice of asking, listening, looking and interpreting fed into my portrait photography for the general public. I began to ask who and what the pictures were for, and then in collaboration we would produce such different views as seemed feasible, or as the sitters gave themselves permission to show to me.

It was only years later when I was in therapy and trying to 'speak' to various interior parts of myself that I began to make connections with this earlier practice and seek for a way of portraying psychic images of myself.

But this is to jump ahead. The photos that follow illustrate the work I did in my high street photography years. Weddings, portraits, family groups and baby photos were my bread and butter, with passport pictures – remember this was in the days before photo booths – as petty cash. More out of the ordinary was the work with actors and actresses, modelling portfolios, and legal work.

For many women, their
wedding day is one of life's
most spectacular events,
often staged in order for the
woman to be dressed up,
looked at and photographed.
For photographers,
wedding pictures are
probably the most routine
job, often referred to as good
money-spinners.

The empty signifier?

In all the years I ran a studio, no 'father and child' portraits were ever commissioned.

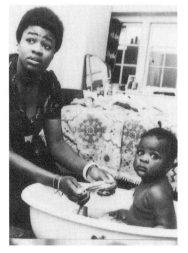

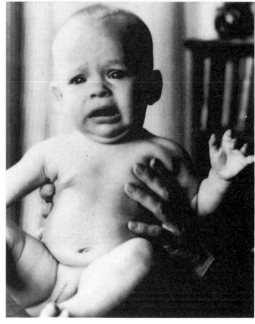

These are not real but imaginary children, conjured out of the skills of the photographer, in collusion with parents.

It is sometimes necessary to take up to thirty different pictures in order to get a family group where everyone will 'look good'.

Bread and butter work always included some legal photography. Here, to demonstrate the type of picture needed, the commissioning solicitor lies on the grass in the cemetery where his client had been struck down by the falling headstone on her husband's grave.

I always enjoyed producing portraits that made my sitters feel happy with themselves, at the same time as they fulfilled the purpose for which they were done. The women here are from a range of social backgrounds, each with different uses for my work. Which one had married two revolutionary leaders and which had brought up her daughter single-handed? Although I did what was required of me at the time, there is no way of telling from the images.

Modelling portofolios were often shot out of doors. The types of women who commissioned me were invariably looking for a 'romantic' approach at that time.

Working with actors and actresses always stretched me. I spent several hours doing a session, often with changes of clothes and location. We worked jointly to produce images which their agents could use to sell them to television, film or theatre companies. Over the years I worked for some clients on an annual basis, for their yearly change of image in *Spotlight* casting directory. How they presented themselves to me would vary depending upon their feel of the 'market forces' at any given moment. Sometimes we would take shots 'in character' or in the style of a period. Sometimes I would produce several distinct images from one sitting, sometimes we would just look for the 'best' one.

A character actress in full flow.

*Actor Neil Kennedy: a
range of images taken across
a period of six years.*

*Nigerian actor and
playwright Jemi Ajibade.*

I often photographed people for the surrealist painter Jas Wood, amongst them Cherie Cleary. Jas used my photos as the basis for his work and then asked Cherie to add her own comments and marks when the painting was partly finished. One day I asked Cherie to go to a photo booth on her way to visit me and also to bring me a typical snapshot of herself. I was becoming more and more intrigued by my ability to produce visual myths. It was not that I was seeking the 'real' Cherie (an impossibility), but that I had begun to realise that the problem of how to represent somebody was far greater and more complex than I had ever imagined. How to do it when a third party had commissioned the image only compounded the problem.

PUBLIC IMAGES: PRIVATE FUNCTIONS
Ed Barber talking to Jo Spence

ED BARBER: To start with, can we talk about your view of high street portraiture?

JO SPENCE: As far as I can see, it hasn't changed all that much from when I was a high street photographer fifteen years ago. All that has changed is perhaps the heightened use of technology. For instance, I used tungsten lamps where people use electronic flash now, and we have winders instead of knobs in the side of cameras and the speed of the film has increased. But basically the unit you mostly work with is an empty box with a bit of glass in front, and with light-sensitized material at the back. Working in the studio is just the same – you start with an empty space and gradually add things in. The technology in respect of colour is, of course, incredibly different from black and white, but I think styles of photography just revolve around certain permutated possibilities. When doing a portrait there's a split between what you know is possible and what's available, so people mostly only get what's available.

It's become more sophisticated though – it's now a bit like painting by numbers. But you get what you pay for, and if you happen to live in Deptford then what you are buying is tanta-mount to what you'd have bought in the thirties except that it might be in colour. And if you happen to live in Marylebone then you can commission somebody to photograph you to look like a Rembrandt oil painting – you're buying a particular aesthetic, really.

EB: That's also apparent in the distinction between 'social' portraiture (for the general public) and 'executive' portraiture (for public relations).

JS: Let's put it another way. In the end it's also to do with who's paying the bill, isn't it? How you present the person photographically will change if the sitter isn't paying for the work themselves, if you are not trying to please *them*. In high street photography you have something which you have nowhere else – a direct one-to-one confrontation in which you are present all the way through the transaction and you have to be there to collect the cash at the end. If they don't like it, basically there is no deal.

The history of high street photography could be seen as an impoverished social history of sorts, in the sense that high street photographers are used very much by people to recall particular moments in their lives (rituals if you like); not just weddings. There are usually loads of other things that they have recorded, but we don't have access to most studios' negative files.

EB: How did you develop the necessary social and technical skills?

JS: You learn on the job, evolving a series of techniques based around 'safe' lighting. But I was a kind of warts-and-all photographer working within what I'd call a 'realist' aesthetic, in that I'd try to indicate to clients something of what I thought they were 'really like', at the same time as trying to flatter them. I would do all my flattery at the time through lighting rather than later in the printing, but I would never knife a negative, that was my boast in those days. I took over my studio from a photographer who worked on quarter-plate film and who retouched all his negatives by hand – he thought I was crazy, and very sloppy.

I had one large light source that a lighting-cameraman made for me, thank God, in the first week I was in business. I used it for the rest of my life in the studio. It was a square wooden lighting frame hung onto a old hair-dryer stand, on to which 16×100-watt light bulbs were mounted. This gave me my north light when diffused through a sheet of fibre glass, which I could wheel around the sitter. I also used a spotlight which I had at the back of the studio. I could put this onto a face from afar and by focusing down the beam I could bring up the sitter's cheek bones, or not, depending on how fat the person was. And if I was in a good mood I'd light the background or rim-light the hair. If you actually got on with the person it got you through the photographic session. Whereas if some cold fish came in from the House of Commons I could spend hours lighting the face and clothes because basically I had nothing to say to them. That's what I called my technique!

I had a very uncommercial attitude to photography in the beginning; remembering that I started life as a shorthand-typist in a 'general practitioner' studio it was an amazing leap for me to become a photographer. I realized I knew nothing, but from observations and from reading magazines and photography books I carried this repertoire of images within me, and lo and behold they came out of me in the studio. I can go through countless sets of negatives of sessions of mothers and children and pick out the Madonna and Child endlessly now. There's no way, though, at the time, that I would ever have identified it as such. I was just getting a 'good' shot of the mothers and kids. Most of those negatives I destroyed later because I was so ashamed at what I'd done (ideologically speaking). I had no sense of a process within photography, or of gradually changing my practice, I just wanted it to be 'right' for some authority figure in my head. And later when I was critical of what I'd done, like some naughty child I wanted to destroy the evidence. It's a real shame.

EB: What kind of people did you photograph?

JS: When I started, I really wanted to photograph actors and actresses, so in that sense I was already one step beyond the aspirations of a high street photographer. In fact, though, I'd photograph anyone who came through the door. The pictures I borrowed from Lizette to put outside my studio were all of the pearl-and-twinset type of person, and so they were the kind of people I got in the beginning.

A series of different people started to come in as the pictures changed, like an Indian dancer, a black body builder, and a woman who wanted herself photographed in the nude; they went beyond the images outside. When I put their new icons outside this indicated that I'd shifted my range of photography, and then it also influenced what I was asked to do at the high street level because people thought 'Oh, she's an arty photographer, she will do an artistic number on our family.' I did a Robin Hood act for years because if somebody poor came in I would do a no-nonsense portrait for a couple of quid, and if somebody who appeared to be loaded came in I would do the full number and charge them 40 quid. In the end I had to have a price list printed as I wasn't always good at judging who could afford what. You have to have a good memory to make a good liar.

Then I started doing Hampstead weddings and they were fabulous, because that's just visual anthropology on the move.

You are actually paid to go and watch people's lives and eat their best food and wine. I used to go and perform through a kind of split personality where I would do the expected romantic lovey-dovey stuff and the standard groups that I'd watched other photographers doing outside registry offices. But I was also influenced by Diane Arbus. I was a nasty, sneaky, little rat behind the camera who said: 'I'll show you people what you are really like!' So at a wedding I would be oscillating across those two areas, and then I found that people really liked both types of pictures. Only it wasn't always the same people. So, the wedding couple might like the Diane Arbus shots of their families, and all the mums and dads would pick out the lovey-dovey stuff. But of course I can't illustrate that here or I'd get sued.

People do have a great deal of knowledge of what they want but they don't usually have the nerve to ask for it, or they are sometimes unable to articulate it. My type of clientele didn't want to know how *other* people were. They just wanted themselves to be as idealised as possible while allowing me at the same time to do this sneaky number on the rest of the family. In a way you are being given permission to break through some of the taboos they daren't break themselves. There was often a kind of collusion between me as the photographer and the couple that the families weren't really all that nice. In a way it was the couple using my work, saying things they had never dared to their families. I was good at producing what I can only call caricatures.

EB: Looking back, how did you deal with the directness of that relationship between you and your clients?

JS: I shifted from being a transient photographer of the photographing-people-from-my-phone-number-type to having a permanent address and I suddenly realised that I had to fix all my prints properly, because if they faded the clients were going to come back and moan at you. That was quite a shock.

I remember going to my first wedding – my dad got it from a factory mate whose daughter was getting married. I had to borrow a camera to do it. I said to my dad: 'I will only do it if you set the groups up for me because I don't actually have the nerve to do it.' So we worked as a team – can you believe it? He wasn't that brilliant at it, so all the groups had people hanging off the edges. But I got a lot of money out of it and that money went towards my first camera. In fact, you have to be completely controlling, though you have to appear not to be.

You feel this terrible responsibility for the £10 that you're getting (as it was then). You mustn't fail.

One other thing you're doing in wedding photography is exactly what you're doing in family photography generally, which is to paper over the cracks of the dissent that you see. You expect it with two different families meeting at the wedding, but not when the so-called ideal family comes into the studio. I often got couples coming in with their children and then coming back with their next husband and then coming again with their next set of children.

So there's a kind of cynicism built into that for me. Then you get some families coming in and all you see is a running miserable banter at the child, very often because the child is being told to construct its face for the camera. You're not even intuiting that, they are literally telling the child what not to do in front of the camera. And then a lot also depends on where the power base is in the situation, whether it's the man or woman who can tell the other adult and child what to do.

I've made some terrible blunders by not getting that right – who I take my instructions from. If you take them from the wrong person the others are going to freeze up. There's a series of bribes and threats going on – either the kid's going to get thumped or get a smartie.

I often got so wound up by all this that I used to have a dartboard in the studio at the end I shot from, and I used to put spare prints up on it. When kids came in, I'd let them play darts before they played the photography game, because it was one way of getting the aggro out of them as I knew what was about to come. And I've often stood there and watched a kid put a dart in somebody's eye on the dartboard, then sit down and be a beautiful little Lord Fauntleroy type – conjured up by the mother and me.

I remember asking a five-generation group, from a very small baby to the great-great-grandmother. 'Could you lean in a bit and touch each other?' They froze and one said: 'Oh no, none of that. I don't want her to touch me.' It's not only what they say – you've got to intuit what's possible and what's not. The other easy mistake is when a couple comes to be photographed and you try and get them to be closer. One couple said to me, 'Why are you trying to do all this? We are brother and sister?' These are the things that you literally have to learn on the job. That's aside from the techniques of how to light and how to flatter them and how to get the money out of them and how not to get a brick thrown through the window.

In some instances people's self-image is so low that they don't have any idea at all, and then you've got to work very hard to give them a new fantasy. Which, as I like people, wasn't that difficult. I was striving for a so-called 'human moment', waiting for them to 'reveal' themselves to the camera, which I see as highly problematic now. I believed that there would be an 'essence', a sight of themselves, that *they* knew but nobody else did, that somehow I could make visual. That to me was the basis of my portraiture, and it must have worked, however critical I am of it today, because I got a lot of repeat jobs and recommendations.

EB: I think there is a sort of character revelation which is acceptable, but personally I don't agree with the idea of 'essence/quintessence'.

JS: Oh, it's total rubbish. But because I grew up with a low self-image, I sussed out very quickly that as a photographer I could play the role of cosmetician. To let them see their chin wasn't as grotesque as they thought because it really wasn't. And that they could be photographed in profile because there isn't really any big deal about it. Plus they could also be photographed with their mouth open speaking, laughing – all the things I saw people blocking for the camera because they believed they would not photograph very well. I learnt that from Sydney Weaver who was a humanist. I still see that as a valid act – I think that if somebody can be made a bit happier about how they look, then perhaps they are going to think differently about themselves. But, of course, that won't change the basic society that produced that perception.

And that's not to say I avoided the cliches. During a general election I had a Labour, Tory and Liberal candidate coming in to be done, and that gave me more insight into portrait photography than anything else. The Liberal bloke was an ordinary ex-working class man from the Welsh valleys who came in his barrister's outfit and when I asked him why he said, 'because they want to see that I've made it.' The Labour man came looking like a worker just off the job, though I knew he lived in this posh flat in Hampstead. When I asked him why he wasn't dressed normally, he replied 'Because I have to be a man of the people to my electorate in Yorkshire. But could you not show my bad teeth?' The third guy who came in was the first Lord of Scotland, and he came in looking like a Belsen case because he was so uptight about everything to do with public appearances. The series of pictures of him was diabolical and he said, 'You will have to come up to my house where I am surrounded by my family, because that's the only way I'll relax, and because I want to look like a family man.'

They were not working within class types at all; they were working within power stereotypes which are to do with who they are going to 'sell' their image back to.

I was privileged in photographing actors and actresses. Because they'd been through drama school or whatever, they knew how to hold or literally construct themselves for the camera. Basically they use their facial expressions, their hair, their hands and clothes much more than most people do. People know how to do it in the real world, but they don't know how to do it for the camera. So having learned from that, I could slide a bit of it back into my ordinary sessions of portraiture. I found with photographing actors that if they changed their clothes, everything else changed – they would go into another mood almost, because that's how they work as actors.

EB: Do you think you ever exploited your position as a photographer or do you think you were more sensitive to the needs of people coming into your studio?

JS: I realised very early on that a portrait session is a bit like going to be psychoanalysed – that the sitter feels you have the power to look into them. Which, of course, you don't. So I particularly developed a practice of working with women, in which I would actually treat them as women, as human beings – I wouldn't treat them as sex objects. When I was asked to do a nude photo – the first nude I ever did – I found it very, very difficult to do. Firstly because I was so uptight about my own body, and secondly because I couldn't quite understand why she wanted a nude photograph for her boyfriend which wasn't a pin-up. Consequently, I did what I would call a 'shy woman' portrait, where I minimized the body and yet I think I made her look beautiful. I thought it was a unique and timeless photograph – no one had ever taken a picture like it before. Yet you could go into a library now and slot it into an archive of pictures of the period quite easily.

I had a number of problems photographing women with no clothes on, because of my own ideological problems of looking and fears about my own desires. You project on to the sitter to some extent as a woman. My first male nude was a nightmare too. I just didn't know what to do! When I got a whole spate of work from straight actors who suddenly wanted to be photographed with no clothes on, I was completely freaked out until I found my own style. I did it through humour, which was the only way I could deal with the naked male body: I had one of them running for the bus in his socks with a briefcase.

First published in TEN.8, Winter 1983/4.

CHANGES OF DIRECTION: DOCUMENTARY WORK 1973 TO 1975

During the high street photography period I had access to people who were of a different political persuasion from me. (Although brought up in a socialist household I deemed myself to be a liberal). My boyfriend from 1967 was David Phillips who became a postgraduate student at the London School of Economics in 1968 and was a socialist historian. My part-time printer at the studio, Rick, was in the Communist Party. Between them, they managed to 'educate' me to such an extent that I finally felt that the work I was doing contradicted my political beliefs. I wanted to belong to a more egalitarian society, and felt that the emphasis should be on children's rights. After years of watching children through the back of my camera, literally socialized and 'constructed' for me by a variety of parents into 'ideal children', I felt very definitely on the side of the child. In truth, of course, I was also still very much in touch with the child in myself. As an evacuee during World War 11, I had moved home eleven times and school six times by the time I was ten, and had felt totally powerless most of that time. I got involved in setting up a group called Children's Rights Workshop, and worked there on a voluntary basis. We set up a children's book project and began reviewing picture books for *Spare Rib* and other magazines. We also got interested in the ways photography constructed views of childhood and with an Arts Council grant put an exhibition on the road entitled *Children Photographed* which explored various photographic styles. This was the first exhibition I had anything to do with.

It occurred to me during this period that I could use my camera differently, and that if I worked in the documentary mode I could produce photographs which could be the basis for new reading materials for young children. My first concept was for an alternative children's picture book showing pictures of the secret world of young children early in the morning before the adults were up and about. I abandoned this as unrealistic and began instead to take photographs for a gypsy literacy project. Here I encountered daily the problem of whose reality I was looking at. The ethical problems of my assumed right to photograph others was placed squarely on the agenda at this point and I became convinced that

The Secret World of Children.

At the Children's Rights Workshop I tried to produce children's reading materials based on photographs. To this end I started to do 'A Day in the Life' of the children of Rosemary Stones and Andrew Mann. This involved getting up at 5.30 to wait for Fred and Catherine to wake up, and then following them through their day. It was the most taxing day I had ever spent. It started with wonder and exhilaration, as I 'spied' upon their activities prior to the household rising, and ended with my total exhaustion as they finally went to bed. By that time, they were both totally aware of what I was doing, and were producing cameos for the camera without a word of instruction. At one point Fred told me to take the picture differently from the way I had set it up! I felt that they had both already internalized the idea of narrating their lives. I found it impossible to conceive of stepping outside linear time, or of not working towards a narrative conclusion.

The pictures were never used.

people would be better off taking their own pictures. However, this conviction took no account of the ways in which skills are passed on from professionals to lay people, or of the things that people don't want to show or to talk about. Or have been taught not to remember.

During this period, the first 'people's autobiographies' were being produced in East London. Although photography was peripheral to this project, some of us were asked to produce portraits to accompany people's recollections of their working lives. I also became involved in the women's movement, and started trying to photograph women's work, something which had previously been invisible within visual representation. I began to take photographs of cultural events within the women's movement but had very little notion of why I was doing it beyond the fact that they were 'there'. Many women photographers were gravitating towards *Spare Rib* magazine as an outlet for their work, and although no payment was ever involved we were always pleased to see our work in print, and to be of use to the women's movement.

Gypsies and Travellers

In 1974 while working at the Children's Rights Workshop, I met Terry Dennett. Terry was a socialist earning his living as a scientific photographer whilst doing research into a history of cultural struggles of the British left and teaching photography to children in his spare time.

We started to visit illegal sites in various parts of London where gypsies and travellers were encamped, and to take photographs. You could say that it was the classic introduction to documentary photography for me. I was both privileged and upset to be allowed to look at a world where people worked so hard to survive, whilst labouring under such terrible disadvantages. The transient sites in particular had no plumbing or refuse removal and life appeared to be very hard. I feel in retrospect that I was looking at them sometimes as the exotic 'other', and at other times as 'victims of society'. My picture making process duly reflects this.

In our travels we made contact with Venice Manley, who ran a school for gypsy children on a London site and did occasional teaching on itinerant sites. Through her we began to visit regularly one site in East London and take pictures of the residents. I had no real idea of why I was taking the pictures, but felt a compulsion to keep returning and looking. We always took contact sheets back to the site and provided the people we had photographed with images of themselves. Here I encountered an antagonism to images which were not idealized or obvious snapshots. To attempt to interest people in a sociological approach to their lives seemed impossible. It never occurred to me to teach people to take photographs of their own lives. Later I was asked by the Gypsy Education Council to take some photographs for the purposes of teaching literacy. I began to do this but eventually stopped as I felt totally inadequate to the task. My version of their reality got more and more problematic. In retrospect I can see that although I was a nice liberal humanist, I had no clue as to the history of the gypsy and travelling people, or their real social, economic or political needs. My thanks to them all, though, for helping me to understand my ignorance better.

Working with Terry Dennett, photographing travellers camped under Westway, Notting Hill Gate, London.

*Heroines or Victims? How
to move beyond the
stereotypes?*

Many children positively revelled in being photographed. But not all. . .

My journey through documentary photography took a classic form. I started on the edges of an unknown sector of society, gradually moving closer and closer to the 'inside' where I was allowed to observe ancient customs like cockfighting. The 'romantic photographic eye' proceeded in parallel.

I became obsessed with observing the social ways in which women conducted their housework. The site, though bare, provided close access, and work and play often went on alongside each other. At least this is what I thought I saw.

A typical 'camera club' shot in the guise of documentary photography.

Moving, finally, to the most affluent and organized area of the life of travelling people, I was trusted to accompany Venice onto the downs at Epsom. Here the ultimate accolade was accorded me . . . I was allowed inside a gypsy home. So many times I have heard documentary photographers, the outsider with a camera, the do-gooding helper with the extra eye, discuss tactics of how to penetrate and intervene, unasked, into the lives of others. Later to sell their version of that reality to a third party. How much simpler to pass on skills! But where does political analysis come from? Who is to say who is oppressed by whom? Who is to make the choice of which ways the world needs to change?

Working Lives

*In the mid-seventies
Centerprise publishing
project and bookshop was
set up in Hackney in East
London. As a local
photographer I was pleased
to be invited, along with
Terry Dennett and many
others, to produce portraits
which could be used in a
book of oral histories of
local residents. For the first
volume we were asked to
produce single images, but
for the subsequent volume
we were encouraged to spend
more time with our subjects
and try to translate their
lives into a series of pictures.
A travelling exhibition
came out of this (in which I
played a* tiny *part) called*
Working Lives.

Invisible Labour

I began photographing women's labour as part of my contribution to the exhibition Women and Work. *To glimpse working class women at their 'daily toil' was for me a way of reclaiming my own mother's identity, and allying myself to it, for here was the world in which she had occupied a place. I began to be aware of my middle classness on this project, and to feel quite uncomfortable with it.*

*Trying to show women's
invisible labour.*

Women Musicians

I began to take photographs of cultural events in the women's movement and was enthused by my first sight of an all-women group of musicians. This was not part of my own reality though, and I was being pulled towards the emerging debates around photographic theory. Such debates seemed to be problematizing documentary photography and I wanted to explore what was being discussed. I stopped taking documentary photographs almost as suddenly as I'd started.

PHOTOGRAPHY WORKSHOP 1974 ONWARDS

Terry Dennett and Jo Spence

We founded Photography Workshop in 1974 as an independent educational research, publishing and resource project. In 1980 it became a registered charity and non-profit-making limited company. And it is still going strong today. To avoid becoming overwhelmed by the bureaucratic concerns associated with running an organisation we agreed to run the workshop on a voluntary basis. In this way we have been able to limit our overheads, cut office work to the minimum and direct the maximum finance towards the Workshop's goals. Because there were no monetary rewards at issue we have never had to involve ourselves with the petty individualism and power struggles that have devastated other groups. Nor have we had to spend half our time writing out grant applications and being interviewed by funding bodies. The Workshop is run with the same dedication and enthusiasm as 'advanced hobbyists' devote to their subject. Additional advantages and resources have come from the decision to set up the Workshop's archive on the basis of the extensive collections of material already owned by its members and research associates. In practice this means that the *use* of a wide range of material has been assigned to the Workshop, but the various owners/custodians still retain control.

Over the years, various individual projects have been systematized into a programme which offers a critical 'use value' model of photographic practice and investigation, in contrast to much institutionalized photo practice which is still largely concerned with status (radical or otherwise), certification, and what might be termed 'commodity values'.

Like many groups which emerged in the 1970s, Photography Workshop began by producing exhibitions in the 1930s documentary mode, similar to that of the Farm Security Administration and the *Picture Post* photographers. Exposure to the work of the prewar German left Arbeiterfoto groups and to John Heartfield led to our abandoning the documentary mode in favour of montage and the non-naturalistic methods of cartoons, theatre and music-drama (see *Re-modelling Photo History*). Current exhibitions, like *The Picture of Health?*, often revolve around biographic

A 'Welliflex' camera.

and autobiographic structures or 'life histories' of individuals or particular incidents. The structure, nature and use of the exhibition has itself become one of our research projects.

We have constantly tried to make our ideas visible. Members involved in research projects have systematically published their findings, while others have set up or collaborated in teaching workshops, lectured throughout London and the home counties, and used slide shows to make accessible a variety of differing approaches to photography. Small teaching exhibitions (many of which can be interchanged or juxtaposed to suit particular needs), have gone on show in art centres, community and youth projects, weekend and day schools and at conferences, as well as within a whole range of formal and informal teaching situations.

Over the years the work has settled into three main areas aimed at establishing a collection of progressive alternative materials on photography. These areas cover questions of ideology, technology and past cultural and political struggles, all of which are invisible in standard histories of photography. An example from the technology area is our 'Survival Photography' project in which we interweave academic research with our concern to encourage a self-reliant, non-fetishistic, low-cost approach to the tools and materials of photography.

This project on alternative photo technology has investigated many common industrial and domestic products and found ways of using them in photography. The Workshop's historical re-searches have brought to light many old processes, formulas and methods which are still useful today. The photo chemical research project has resulted in an indexed collection of 2000 substitutes and alternatives to commercial photo chemicals, plus a subsidiary list of a thousand items which can no 'longer be purchased commercially but can be cheaply made with the formulas we have collected. Several parts of the project have provided material for successful workshops, like 'The Home Made Camera' children's workshops which resulted in the unforgettable Welliflex and J-Pak cameras. These and similar projects continue to expand, taking on more importance as unemployment rises and economic instability causes further cutbacks in the photographic industry and retail trade.

The Photography Workshop Archive contains the following:

1   Material on the social and technical developments of photo-graphy and related media from 1970 onwards.

2   Material on the history and use of photography in the trade union and labour movements from the 1890s onwards.

3   Copy negatives of archive of the Workers' Film and Photo League, with copies of supporting material, frame stills made from original films, etc.

4   35mm slide collection of contemporary ephemera and adver-tisements concentrating on material useful for discussions of sexism, racism and class bias.

5   Cartoon collection: a) contemporary cartoons from the mass media displaying sexism, racism and class bias for use within

educational and media projects; b) radical and socialist cartoon material from the labour and trade union press.

6   Postcard collection: With this and the cartoon collections we can demonstrate in workshops the mechanism through which cartooning and caricature have their 'effect'. The mode of stereotyping found in both collections highlights certain arguments very effectively when teaching about mediation and the visual representation of social reality. The collection is also a form of social history, particularly of people's life and labour.

Summary of Photography Workshop Aims

● To provide an ongoing photographic research, information and advice resource, and to publish and distribute such research in whatever form is most useful.

● To initiate projects and promote interest in the critical use of photography and various media as educational and communicational tools.

● To encourage self-reliance in photographic users and makers, especially in the investigation of alternative chemical and photo technology, so as to develop an independence from monopolistic companies. (This is an essential first step towards demystifying technology).

● To self-publish concise educational worksheets on aspects of photography, which can eventually be put together as teaching aids. To make available technical and useful information in poster broadsheet and postcard form.

● To continue to participate in the setting up of short-term groups to carry out specific documentary projects, as requested by educational, community and sub-cultural groups. Additionally to act as intermediaries in the exchange of details between those wishing to teach or learn photographic skills.

● To encourage the photographic recording of personal, group and local history by those involved, with or without the assistance of professional photographers.

● To research and collect all available material on progressive applications of photography in order to make available alternative materials to those which presently constitute the history of photography.

WOMEN'S COLLECTIVE WORK 1974 ONWARDS

One project instigated by Photography Workshop in its embryonic days was the drawing together of politicized documentary photographers. From this effort emerged The Hackney Flashers collective, which produced two major projects *Women and Work* and *Who's Holding The Baby?*, followed later by an educational slide pack called *Domestic Labour and Visual Representation*.

The group consisted at various times of the following people, with a range of backgrounds and skills: An Dekker, Terry Dennett, Helen Grace, Sally Greenhill, Liz Heron, Gerda Jager, Neil Martinson, Maggie Millman, Michael Ann Mullen, Maggie Murray, Jini Rawlings, Ruth Barrenbaum, Christine Roche, Annette Soloman, Jo Spence, Arlene Strasberg, Sue Treweek and Julia Vellacott.

Though the group broke up in the early 1980s, informal contact has been maintained by many members.

Excerpts from Liz Heron's article on the Hackney Flashers' exhibitions written at the height of her involvement, explains the aims and experience of working in the group.

HACKNEY FLASHERS COLLECTIVE: WHO'S STILL HOLDING THE CAMERA?

Liz Heron

When a group of North London photographers got together with the aim of organising a joint project because they felt their work was isolated from any social or political context, it was a new step to take. Certainly exhibition projects have been carried out by two or three photographers together, but with only that specific purpose in mind; and of course there are those who express their politics through the work they do for the left and alternative press. The aim of this group, however, was to develop an ongoing activity in the area where they lived and worked, which probably could define it as what has become known as 'community photography' – or rather one of its many varieties. That definition is certainly more applicable to the collective as it was then – four years ago – than now.

Once the group was consolidated it was then a question of what issues to focus on and what form the project would take. The

A typical Hackney Flashers meeting in a member's home.

majority – not all at that stage – were women, and wanted to photograph women in the local area, illuminating some of the inequalities faced outside and in the home. But whether it was to be 'art', information, agit-prop, an exhibition, posters, or published in book-form were still questions – so' was the eventual audience. An opportune solution came along when Hackney Trades Council offered a project: an exhibition of photographs on women at work in the borough as part of its 75th anniversary celebrations '75 years of Brotherhood', (the sisterhood was an afterthought).

Photographs taken for *Women and Work* included women in the professions as well as in office and manual jobs and were accompanied by statistics and other information. To publicly exhibit so many images of women working was an indisputable achievement – such images were rare. The exhibition was well received and has been in constant demand ever since. However there were also inadequacies and in retrospect it seemed to do no more than make a strong statement in favour of equal pay – necessary, but not enough.

Self-criticism wasn't lacking though, for in the process of

preparing the exhibition and sharing skills and ideas, the politics of our feminism had become clearer. There was disparate political experience. Some had been active in left groups and trade unions, some in community politics and some in the women's movement; the group's cohesion was its feminism, even though not everyone agreed on what that was. There were other differences in levels of practical and technical knowledge. I joined about two years ago because I wanted to learn about taking pictures and at the same time have a reason for taking them – to work in a group and explore ideas about how pictures are used. My lack of technical knowledge presented no problems. 'Professionalism' was never an issue. In principle everyone had something to contribute and those with practical skills were willing to give help and encouragement to the others – there were workshops on darkroom techniques, design and layout. By the time *Women and Work* was completed, a graphic designer and an illustrator were also involved. By then too there was a group identity; we had become The Hackney Flashers.

One comment made about the exhibition was taken to heart – there wasn't enough on the difficulties childcare presents for women. A small exhibition on childcare facilities was subsequently produced for the Under-Fives Campaign in the borough. That was instructive – for what it didn't show. The photographs of nurseries and play groups were useful enough, but the real issue was the long list of children waiting for nursery places, and unlikely to get them. Hackney, for example, had a thousand children on its top-priority waiting list for day-care, to say nothing of all the other under-fives who weren't considered to be in desperate need.

It was only when the decision was made to undertake a long-term project on childcare that the difficulty of making it a single issue became clear. The urgency of childcare provision was undeniable but it was recognised that we had to go beyond just supporting the campaign for more nursery places. We had endless meetings where we argued for keeping things simple, for not alienating anyone, for showing what was desperately needed and what could be done, for an overall analysis of motherhood and childcare. Though we had general agreement on what the problems were, we had different emphases: should we focus on the positive aspects of a local community nursery, an analysis of women's oppression in the family or the ideological role of the media?

A comparison of our two exhibitions, *Women and Work* and *Who's Holding the Baby?* demonstrates how much the work of the group has changed. Class is an issue – it generally is for middle-class photographers with a social conscience (the 'poor' and the 'dis-

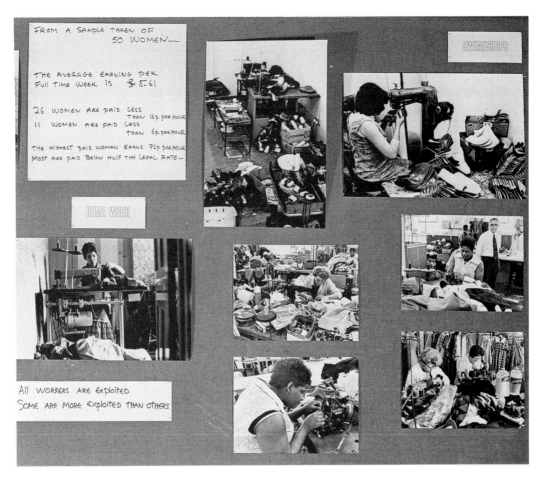

FROM A SAMPLE TAKEN OF
50 WOMEN —

THE AVERAGE EARNING PER
FULL TIME WEEK IS £5·61

26 WOMEN ARE PAID LESS
THAN 16p. PER HOUR
11 WOMEN ARE PAID LESS
THAN 6p. PER HOUR

THE HIGHEST PAID WOMAN EARNS 72p PER HOUR
MOST ARE PAID BELOW HALF THE LEGAL RATE —

SWEATSHOPS

HOME WORK

All WORKERS ARE EXPLOITED
SOME ARE MORE EXPLOITED THAN OTHERS

Women and Work

Panels from the exhibition Women and Work. *The collective's original aim was to document women in Hackney at work inside and outside the home. The intention was to make visible the invisible, thereby validating women's experience and demonstrating their unrecognized contribution to the economy. The limitations of documentary photography became apparent with the completion of this exhibition. The pictures were based on the assumption that the camera was a 'window on the world', and did not question the idea that reality is rooted in appearances.*

UNEMPLOYMENT

MEN & WOMEN   1¼ Million   (August 1975)

1½ Million   ANTICIPATED BY WINTER —

UNEMPLOYMENT FIGURES FOR WOMEN DO NOT REFLECT THE REAL LEVEL OF UNEMPLOYMENT AS THE VAST MAJORITY OF UNEMPLOYED WOMEN ARE NOT REGISTERED AS SUCH AT THE EMPLOYMENT OFFICES.

HACKNEY UNEMPLOYMENT

WOMEN 539

MEN 2907

FOR THE FIRST TIME IN RECENT MEMORY THE LOCAL FIGURES SHOW TWICE AS MANY WOMEN UNEMPLOYED AS THERE ARE REGISTERED VACANCIES.

71.2 % OF WORKERS EARNING LESS THAN £30.00 A WEEK ARE WOMEN —

Freehold

FOR SALE

0·75 Acre Industrial Site with Existing Buildings

Hampton & Sons

6, Arlington Street, SW1.

01·493 8222

advantaged' have been camera fodder almost throughout the history of photography), but we've moved away from just doing documentary exposés of the 'real condition' (which is not to say that they aren't useful in campaigns for better housing, social services etc.) What we've been more explicit about is the necessity for fighting class oppression as well as women's oppression and showing the two as mutually reinforcing.

Women's position in the family is central. Women have the subordinate role of servicing the wage labourer and reproducing the future labour force. But as well as being domestic labourers, women are also wage labourers. Capitalism attempts to deal with this contradiction by continuing to treat women as economically dependent on men and as having the primary role of wives and mothers, while managing (despite legislation) to conveniently maintain women as the cut-price section of the labour force, concentrated in low-paid and unskilled jobs. Women's struggles around equal pay, childcare, abortion, contraception and other issues are of crucial importance in undermining the ideologies of femininity and domesticity. By challenging their subordinate roles not only in the family but also in the hierarchy of labour, women are also attacking the class structures of capitalist society.

It is possible that capitalism could incorporate other forms of the family, but it is the ideology that supports it in its present form which we have to challenge. As women, we learn about ourselves through the family and the education system, and also through the images of ourselves that society holds up to us; but much of women's lived experience is absent from those images. *Women and Work* attempted to attack stereotyped images by concentrating on those areas of women's lives which are usually invisible. But though they were alternative images, they were unable to contradict the dominant notions of women's role in our society because of their form. *Women and Work* was a series of black and white photographs; it used naturalism, the 'window on the world' technique, assuming transparency; but the visible world doesn't so easily yield up the reality of power relationships and institutions. In order to challenge images that serve to maintain women's subordination it is necessary to question the ideas and myths behind such images. For example, a working class woman may recognize herself in a photograph of a woman working in a factory. While her self-recognition is important in terms of validating individual lived experience, it cannot negate the power of what advertising and other media images represent as social reality. These images are not simply a distortion of how we 'really' are, but are part of a process of constructing us and prescribing our feminine role. In *Who's Holding the Baby?* we tried to subvert images and question their meaning through the use of collage and montage. We first saw the possibilities of this when we discussed how two sets of slide images could be used together, one of media images collected and classified by a group member, the other from *Women and Work* which was used as a basis for discussions at meetings and conferences. A workshop produced our first collective efforts: a photograph of a woman working in a garment factory juxtaposed with an advertisement showing a glamorous evening dress with a three-figure price tag. It became increasingly clear that the context in which an image was used could dramatically alter its meaning.

Though images of women varying according to class – downmarket and upmarket products demand different images of femininity – images of women consistently cut across class differences and disguise them. The common roles of wife and mother create the illusion of shared experience, though women may differ vastly in their degree of economic manoeuvrability. One panel from *Who's Holding the Baby?* showing a nanny, an au pair, a childminder, and a mother, each with children, attempted to point out that money (or the lack of it) can make motherhood an easier or more difficult reality. Economic privilege is neglected in newspaper and magazine stories about famous and wealthy women where as wife, mother or daughter, their experiences of the joys and sorrows of family life are equated with a day in Mrs. Average's life; the message is that be it in palace or council flat, the 'female condition' is universal. We are not denying that middle class women are also oppressed by their subordination to men and the gender-based discrimination they encounter, but we are attempting to expose the class differences that are usually hidden in representations of family life.

The ideology of motherhood is one of the things we attempted to expose in *Who's Holding the Baby?*. A collage of consumer goods answered the question 'What are mothers made of?' Panels contrasted photographs of wartime provision for children whose mothers worked in the factories with contemporary photographs of children playing unsupervised, because official policy has now relocated women in the home, although in reality they're still in the factories. We used speech bubbles with a photograph of a homeworker and her child to give information about her pitifully low piecework earnings. Invisible not only in imagery but also in employment statistics, these women are a hidden category of workers, forced to do this kind of work because they need the money, forced to stay at home to look after children.

We tried to question the 'unchangeability' of motherhood by demonstrating that there are alternative possibilities for looking after children like collective childcare and childcare shared by men and women, and by giving information about the campaigns

**Early Attempts at
Photo Montage**

around nurseries, abortion and contraception, violence against women, and other related issues. The section made up of photographs and interviews with the families involved in the Market Nursery revealed a network of support in coping with problems like homelessness, illness, poor housing, unemployment and the difficulties experienced by the growing numbers of single-parent families. Though we did not see the Market Nursery as a solution, there was a strong feeling among some members of the collective that it was vital to document a successful example of united action around childcare provision. Even though it was only on the level of making demands on the Council for funding, it was also about taking control.

Excerpts from an article first published in
PHOTOGRAPHY/POLITICS: I, 1979.

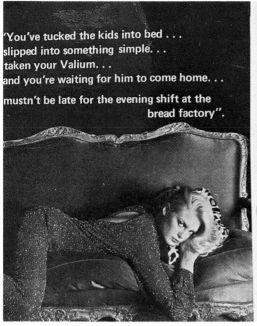

"You've tucked the kids into bed . . .
slipped into something simple. . .
taken your Valium. . .
and you're waiting for him to come home. . .

mustn't be late for the evening shift at the
bread factory".

Hands. Seen almost as soon as
your face. On show. Touching. Holding.
Loving.
  Nail polish is as important as make-up.
That's why we call Cutex the make-up
for nails.
  Thirty different colours. Some
dramatic. Some soft. Some vivid.
Some gentle.
  More than nail polish.
It's make-up for nails.

Cutex

Thirty colours. Some so pearl it's like
dipping your fingers in coloured frost.

Who's holding the baby?

**An exhibition on childcare
by the Hackney Flashers Collective
1978**

We began to juxtapose our naturalistic photographs of women working with product information from adverts for a slide show which developed from Women and Work. *We* also began to use montage. This way we felt we could better indicate the contradiction between women's experience and its representation in the media. We also wanted to raise the question of class, so heavily obscured in the idea of women's experience as universal.

Who's Holding The Baby?
Panels from Who's Holding The Baby? *Women are usually represented as passive suffering victims, unable to find their own solution. We wanted to show women* taking collective action. We used images in different ways: with our own words; with the words of the people we photographed; with the media's words.

Market Nursery, Hackney

"When I started coming here
Andrew was 11½m, and we lived in
a second floor flat with no
garden. The other two children
were going to a day nursery -
proper council one. It was
great - but you can't go there
and stay. They don't want
parents there - you have to
leave your kid and go. It's
more friendly and helpful here."

"Definitely we need much more
places for under 5's. Mums
should go out and mix with
others. If you have them at
home with you all the time
they're very, very, difficult
when they have to go to school.
They wont let their mums go,
see! Anyway, some mothers
have to go out to work."

ESME ROBERTS

This image was entirely constructed and had nothing to do with documentary photography. We graffitied the wall late one night, then photographed it. A photograph of the mother and children was laid underneath a hole cut in the print of the wall. Then a banner headline was added. Thus the link could be made between the WHY of struggles for childcare facilities, and the HOW.

D ISRUPTING SEXUAL STEREOTYPES
1977

I shared an interest in gender, sexuality and portraiture with Ed Barber, one of the people I worked with at Half Moon Photography Workshop and on the magazine *Camerawork*.

Using the same backdrop and lighting as in my Hampstead studio and a 35mm camera with black and white film, we invited actor Neil Kennedy to re-style Alan Rebbeck for the camera shortly before he appeared on stage as a pantomime dame.

The politics of sexuality brought with it a whole host of fears for me. De-naturalizing sexuality meant facing the long held-at-bay limitations of the ways in which I lived out and negotiated my own sexuality. The project also strengthened my interest in theory.

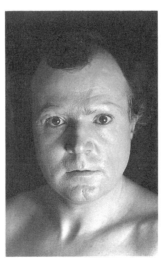

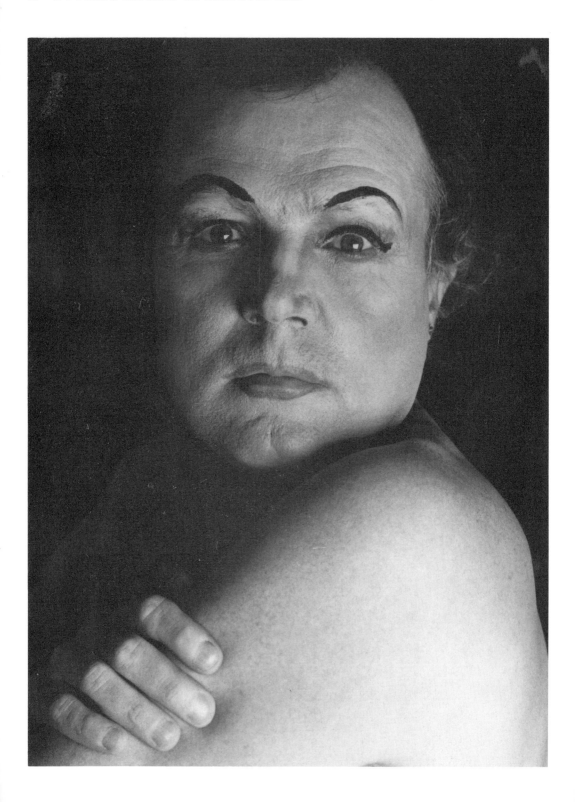

VISUAL AUTOBIOGRAPHY: BEYOND THE FAMILY ALBUM 1979

The exhibition *Beyond the Family Album* was made specifically for inclusion in the *Three Perspectives on Photography* exhibition held at the Hayward Gallery in 1979. I had never been asked to produce work for use in a gallery before and had no idea what to expect when I showed it. In it I turned to an investigation of my own family and my class background, and what it meant to be a woman. The cross fertilization between class and sexuality has informed all my work since this period.

As a photographer I had spent most of my working life trying to visually represent other people. When I reached forty, working as a freelance documentary photographer and becoming more politicized, I began to have serious doubts about whether to continue with my work. I questioned my right to act on behalf of those I photographed, who had no control over what was done with their images. I questioned naturalism as the best way to use photography politically. Feminism had made me aware of my socialization as a woman and of the process of 'bourgeoisification' which had taken me away from the working class roots and struggles of my own family. As a result I began to think about how I had been represented by others.

This was the starting point of a project on 'my history' which I began by tentatively examining photographs of myself and ended by taking control over how I wanted to be photographed. Thus I changed my role from being behind the camera to being in front of it and became at the same time an active rather than passive subject. Not only did I take more control over what I presented of myself to the camera, but I also decided what techniques I wanted used on me.

In my early photographs there is no record of my appalling health (or the many doctors who fobbed me off with under-developed medicines because of my unseen 'social problems'); no record of the pointless years shunted around schools inside formal education (where I was downgraded for 'unruly behaviour', constantly evaluated and eventually crushed into the mould of 'typist'); no record of a broken marriage and the havoc this so-called failure caused me; no record of hard work done for countless employers; no record of trying to please parents and

other authority figures; no record of struggles. . . Moreover, those 'happy', 'serious', 'loving', 'miserable', but always passive visual moments which do exist, those moments which only show surface information about me, give no indication at all of the wider social, economic and political histories of our disgusting class-divided society. They are rendered invisible within my 'family album'. (But then this is normal to most families, who are encouraged only to photograph their leisure, their consumption, or their ownership and to show the 'harmony' of their lives.)

Showing at the Hayward Gallery in 1979 was a totally alienating experience.

I began to reverse the process of the way I had been constructed as a woman by deconstructing myself visually in an attempt to identify the process by which I had been 'put together'. Through this I was able to understand what my photographs didn't show: the manner in which I had moved entirely away from any knowledge or belief in a wider grouping of people, locked as I had been in a private struggle to come to terms with my own 'feminin-ity' and with the fragmented role-playing this entails. As a socialist I saw that I still lacked a coherent understanding of myself in terms of objective class reality. And I realized that I had to reject the whole of my learned photographic practice because it had made me visually represent others in ways not necessarily in their class interests in order to earn my living as a photographer.

I feel it has been useful to allow this material to be used; it no longer seems to have very much to do with 'me', as a person, but rather has become a repository of various conventional techniques and choices within photography.

I still feel that the personal is political. There is no way I could have understood fully the political implications of trying to represent other people (however well intentioned) if I had not first of all begun to explore how I had built a view of myself through other people's representations of me.

1

2

THE FAMILY ALBUM
1939 to 1979

1 Eight and a half months
*(High street photographer –
Woodford)*

2 Five hundred and twen-
ty eight months later

TRYING to recall one's own history is a painful process of selective remembering and selective forgetting. Of knowing and not knowing. At times moving from description to sentiment, from self pity to self evaluation. I have tried not to treat myself as an object under the microscope, as a sociologist or anthropologist might, nor to pretend with hindsight, that I was always in control of my life. Quite clearly I was never in control.

My parents, Herbert Cyril Clode and Gladys Kate Peach married in 1933 during the Depression. I was born in June 1934. These early photographs, all taken before I started school, show me as the centre of the family. My mother, who stayed at home to look after me, dearly loved my father who worked in a furniture store in Putney, in order to support us all.

Both my parents came from working class families. My paternal grandfather had a history of militancy in the Transport and General Workers' Union. My parents, during the early part of their lives together, were in a process of what has comed to be termed 'social mobility', moving from one class to another. For as long as I can remember we lived in 'nice' suburbs of London. Before I went to school my father had taught me to read, write and count, and to use the telephone.

As a record of *her* life, as a mother, these early photographs give no indication of the amount of sheer hard work involved in childcare.

Of my father's life as a worker I had no record at all.

1 Three weeks old: a bundle in a basket. Who is she? Who took the picture?

2 Fourteen months: we look very pretty together, artistically posed in this 'mother and child' cameo on the Bognor beach (*father, deceased/snapshot*)

3 Three years: in grandma's back yard, Colliers Wood. 'Such a lovely little girl, doesn't she look like Shirley Temple?' (*Uncle Syd, deceased/ 'amateur' photographer*)

4 Four years: visit to Broadstairs. My mother was pregnant; did I know? (*Sunbeam Photo Company Ltd/beach photographer*)

5 Four years, two months: the last record of having my mother to myself, in our garden in Wandsworth. She seems to have looked after me well. At this time the peace treaty was being signed between Hitler and Chamberlain. (*father/snapshot*)

'GEMINI. . . Mars increases your drive and energy after the 16th, and the people you meet now may have a profound influence on your attitudes and beliefs. . .'
'My' horoscope *Women's World*, May 1979

WHY would I want to put my 'private' photographs on show for everybody to see? Maybe it is because this record of my life lacks so much that I want to share its gaping holes with others.

When World War II broke out it altered most British people's lives. For me, it happened just as I was about to start school – the very same week. Almost immediately, my mother, our new baby and I were evacuated to Surrey. My father visited us at weekends, until the panic was over and we returned home.

In 1940 I was sent from London, this time alone and even further away. I lived for a while with a family of Cornish agricultural workers, sharing a room with another unhappy child. Later my mother rescued me from an isolation hospital where I had been sent with 'skin trouble'. A week after I was back in the bosom of the family it cleared up. For a while, before going into a munitions factory, my father was a rent collector. Ironically, during this time we were homeless and lived with my grandparents. At some point we moved to a suburban estate with ornamental cherry trees and front gardens with no fences. By now both parents were working in essential warwork, contributing to the 'war effort'. My brother was in a nursery and I became a 'latch key' child.

In 1944 my brother and I were evacuated together, this time being sent unwillingly to a Derbyshire mill village where we lived with a family of coal miners. I became a surrogate parent for my brother; a role which we both resented but were trapped in. No photographs exist of this period, but the iniquities dealt out to evacuees certainly need some form of documentation. During this period I experienced incredible friendship from other children similarly 'lost', like myself. We felt the adults had abandoned us.

Clearly these recollections hardly transcend anecdote but to me they are an essential part of my 'memories'.

2

3

4

1 Five years: displaced from the centre of the family. And showing it. For me this year meant having a baby brother, starting school, war breaking out, being evacuated. What will happen to this ideal family, in this idyllic garden? My father's age, flat feet and piles, prevented his call up.
(*grandfather, deceased/ snapshot*)

2 Five years: 'mother's little helper' walking brother Michael in the park.
(*mother, deceased/snapshot*)

3 Six years: looking like an uncared for, but rather cheeky 'orphan'. This is a 'face' I still see on me even now. Less often though.
(*school photograph/Cornwall*)

4 Eleven years: looking like a refugee. Another 'face' I still see on me . . . more often now. The five year gap between these photographs masks years of being constantly uprooted, adapting, being ill, living in different families, various schools, sleeping in street shelters. Being the one to get home before everybody else and preparing the evening meal. Resenting the loss of my so-called childhood, but becoming independent and able to cope at a very early age. From the state's point of view I was another 'problem' which needed solving at various points in this life.

But I never got caught stealing.
(*school photograph/unknown*)

BOTH parents continued to work in factories after the war. We remained suspended, mid class, our process of social mobility halted in flight. We took on the trappings of the deadly lower middle class, respectably waiting for the next generation to move on.

In spite of my repeated attempts to leave home, we remained together as a family. My father forbade me to go ('Why would you want to leave home when you live in London with your family? You know you can't look after yourself properly.') I agreed to stay. We had a family group taken of our 'happy days' together.

At this time I worked as a shorthand-typist in a commercial photographers in Hampstead. The two years' private schooling as a last minute rescue attempt after exam failures in mid teens, had paid off. Here I had access to both the process of being photographed, and to people taking photographs to earn a living.

This was a time of exploration, of boyfriends, of trying desperately to be pretty, of repressed sexuality. I was expected to 'behave' myself with boys. Sometimes I wore white gloves and stockings. Sometimes I still climbed trees.

This ambivalence of wanting to be loved, yet wanting to break away from my family, caused constant tension. Constant asthma. Constant restraint in the name of love.

As my father had 'failed' to get his old job back, I continued to blame him for not trying hard enough. I was arrogant in my ignorance. I had my own problems: I obviously needed to develop a 'personality' to compensate for my lack of beauty. I needed no compensation for my big tits – but didn't know what to do but to hide them.

I saw work as an escape from home life. It was a place to earn enough money for clothes, meet boys (later men). I felt myself lucky to be working in an atmosphere where, although typing letters and balancing accounts all day, I felt something exciting was happening. I never thought of a career for myself. It seemed natural that I earned less than anyone else there. And besides we were all given nice presents at Christmas.

1 Seventeen years: looking glamorous in the back garden. I never worked on the garden but it makes a good backdrop.
(*brother/snapshot*)

2 Eighteen years: Who owns this room in which we pose? Why was this picture taken and sent to friends and family as a Christmas card? Why not a picture of my parents at work in the Tilley Lamp Company in Hendon? This company produced hurricane lamps. When profits fell the owners took the entire factory and offices to Ireland where the government was offering tax incentives.
(*Peter Urry/apprentice photographer/boyfriend*)

3 Offering myself to the camera with a variation of 'The Look'.
(*Peter Urry*)

4 Self portrait in the front room mirror with my first reflex camera. I hadn't got used to the focussing.

5 Playing at being a photographer, in between typing letters.
(*Michael Balfre/apprentice photographer/friend*)

MORE pictures of my face More ritual displaying for posterity. How did I learn how to hold my head, or to lean with hand on hip? To pout prettily? I learned to know every fault on my face, every flaw in my body.

By the time I was twenty I had already been in love with the homosexual boy-next-door, and seduced by a Palestinian guerilla. I became engaged to a Polish sculptor. It was a 'sophisticated' relationship, by which I mean I got fucked regularly. My mother knew, and she worried. But she never spoke.

I saw in him a tragic, romantic figure. Struggling from the past in which he had been snatched from his family by Nazi troops as Poland was invaded. I saw myself as filling the void in him, looking after him, bearing his child. Unknowingly I was dragged into his divorce case, cited as correspondent, and then awarded custody of his existing child. I fled. My parents never knew.

My lack of sex instruction was a nightmare. Loving, and 'giving in', had little to do with the diagrams of reproductive organs offered to me at school. 'Love' meant escape. In Kingsbury my parents continued to struggle. For my part I contributed to family life by catching the last train home each night, creeping in so as not to waken my brother whose room I still shared.

This period of continued surveillance by my parents was for me unbearable. It was unbearable for them, too, but also an expression of their love for me.

1   Twenty years: a 'dirty weekend' at Brighton. No toy panda to sit on, no pretty mother to frame me on the beach. She's there in my head though. I wonder if she and my father ever did this.

2   Another version of 'the look' in Hyde Park. The dark glasses were an affectation which helped to make me feel 'glamorous'.

3   Twenty one years: My first proper studio portrait as a grown up. Taken on a plate camera, carefully lit and posed. The bags under my eyes were removed without my requesting it, the nose slightly 'straightened'. I wore make up specially for this picture and had my hair blonde-streaked. I met the photographer at the local Camera Club.
(*Sydney Weaver, deceased/ photographer/friend*)

4   Twenty four: a glamour session in the studio after-work. The harsh, bleached out lighting makes it look like a press picture. This was my Petula Clark phase. The low necked jumper has been cropped at the shoulder so that it is not too revealing. I never showed it to my parents until much later.

Although three days separate these two pictures my head is held in the same vice-like tilt as in the previous shot. Nobody asked me to do this. I knew from looking in the mirror what angle suited my face best. I had by now spent a lot of time watching other people being photographed. Years later when sitters came to my portrait studio I discovered they also invariably knew the 'best angle' to be photographed from.
(*Michael Balfre/ photographer/friend*)

THE PERIOD of greatest independence. I defied my father at last, and left home. My mother, wringing her hands, crying, wondering where she went wrong. My father telling me never to come back if I was deserting the family.

They said I was in need of care and protection. As it happened, I was.

I was ill for a month, with asthma. Lungs knotted with tension and fear. Later, when I was on a course of new wonder-drugs, the steroid side-effects caused a 14lb tumour on my ovary. After its removal the doctor told me not to worry. My chances of conception had been only cut in half. I worried for years about my 'incompleteness', about my possible lack of 'femininity'.

Working now in various jobs within photography, the time consumed by this growing interest conflicted with my love life. The men I had loved took no interest whatsoever in my work, wrapped up as they were in their own various jobs of policeman, welder, actor, crook. At thirty it was all resolved. I married an ex-sailor who needed a mother. We were both unable to cope with marriage and parted on Guy Fawkes Day two years later. I took the cat with me.

I became a secretary again.

1

2

1 Twenty nine years: a last fling at being 'beautiful'. Still recovering from a major operation, this was taken during a tiring walk on Hampstead Heath.

By now I had learnt to tip my head back slightly (saves retouching), and to smile in a way which hid my dreadful teeth.
(*Michael Wynne/actor/ boyfriend/snapshot*)

2 Thirty years: the marriage. My bouquet came off the Hampstead registrar's window sill. The honeymoon was the most boring holiday either of us had ever had. There is no record of it. After the wedding our respective mothers conceded (at last) that we lived together. Now they could visit us. I wonder about my own mother's sex life. Did she still have one? Did she ever have one?

Years later I was to be a regular photographer at this same registry office, posing people into tidy groups, waiting for brides to smile. Asking them to delay throwing the confetti until I had reloaded my camera. I made a lot of money like this. My ex-husband died of cancer in 1986.
(*David Noble/wedding photographer/friend*)

THIS period sounds like a soap opera as I write it . . . Received back into the arms of my parents, consoling me on my 'failure', I then eloped with an ageing disc jockey who worked for a pirate radio station on the North Sea. Swearing eternal love for me, and leaving behind the sacks of fanmail, we ran off to live in Southern Ireland. We lived on his accumulated earnings in romantic, if somewhat primitive, isolation. While he wrote plays, I planted potatoes, walked the cat, and photographed our neighbours. I enjoyed the fun of washing my films and prints in the running stream as they walked past on their way to the fields; it seemed like a kind of magic to be producing photographs in the middle of nowhere with only the kitchen as a darkroom and no running water. My photographs were rejected by the people whom I depicted; they said they wanted to be shown in their best clothes, not all dirty, doing work.

When winter fell, and the mist settled on our hillside, I was shipped back to London with asthma, bronchitis, and 'psychiatric problems'.

The realization of the impossibility of what we'd tried to do only hit me later. I had tried to create the beginnings of another family unit, I had felt compelled to behave 'normally'. But I hated the constraints, the financial dependence, and continual demand for service.

Whilst struggling to recover, drugged with antibiotics and librium, an old friend virtually forced me to take over his portrait studio in Hampstead, and to become a photographer again. I never forgot this extraordinary act of kindness.

This type of high street photography virtually meant learning on the job, solving whatever problems presented themselves. My first job was to document a graveyard accident for a legal case . . . my last, seven years later, was to make portraits of the children of a man who was big in oil. I learned to be charming and manipulate people. I enjoyed watching and being paid for it.

I fell in love with a student of political science who lived in a room overlooking my studio. I moved in between his unwashed sheets. . . . We drank Dubonnet, stayed together for five years, and remained friends until his death.

1   Two heads held together, mine above his, symbolize the way in which the photographer 'saw' the relationship between us. He couldn't have been more correct as it turned out. My face (but not his) has been retouched, on the print. The day after this was taken we left for our new life in Ireland.
(*Sydney Weaver/photographer/ friend*)

2   Back in the 'real world' of work: I was commissioned to take photographs of 500 international lawyers. On a day trip out with this conference I ended up with a picture of my boyfriend and myself; Windsor Castle is behind us.

Nine years younger than me, David nonetheless, taught me to get less caught up in pointless neurotic patterns of behaviour, by his own love and tolerance.

I was depressed for a year, and tranquillized, because I felt it would soon be too late to 'have a child', (recommended by so many doctors as the cure for illness). These two portraits seem to confirm my compulsion to be part of a couple, and also the need to record the fact.

David died in 1983; he was drowned at Dover.
(*Michael Balfre/ photographer/friend*)

3   Self portrait in my own studio, playing about in between sessions of work. I used this as my Christmas card.

DURING this period both my parents died suddenly. They were worn out, and totally misunderstood by me. For most of my adult life I had learned to 'blame' them for what we had 'lacked' materially as a family; for what they never taught me; for my illnesses (which had become a means of getting attention or controlling difficult situations); for their respectability.

During their lifetime I had never really known either of them. Nor known that they too were caught up in *their* learned assumptions about themselves. My mother though oppressed in many ways as a woman, had always shared everything with my father – the work, the money, the illnesses, the responsibilities. Their real oppression came from the objective class position

they occupied. Standing further away from my personal and highly emotional relationships with them, it became clear that they never had freedom to choose how they lived their lives or brought up their children. It wasn't so much a question of their 'failure' as parents or as people, but that most of their lives had been governed by the ways in which they were forced to sell their labour, rent accommodation, their continual striving to maintain failing health, and the schools, the doctors, the resources they had access to.

The Rent Act in 1959, which had rendered them potentially homeless, had forced them to buy their small flat. Obsessed with the idea of paying off this debt before retiring, they hardly had time to enjoy

the 'security' it gave them. My mother died at 62. My father worked until he was 70 and had one year's retirement before he died, three weeks after my mother.

At the time of their deaths they were between them suffering from arthritis, cancer, bronchitis, asthma, hardening of the arteries, and a constantly slipping disc. They were both on tranquillizers for the latter part of their lives, and sometimes sleeping tablets.

As she was dying, sitting at the kitchen window, overlooking her beautiful garden, I knew she was glad she had died before my father. She had dreaded being left on her own.

My brother and I sold their home. With some of this money I was able to

travel abroad for the first time. It also bought me the privilege of time to reflect and not have to go to work for a whole year. During this time I realized how totally ignorant I was about most things, beyond the views that family, mass media and state schooling had given me. This acceptance of my ignorance (and of my strengths) was a major step towards repairing my own damaged health. My ignorance forced me to look for more coherent ways of understanding our class society. I knew then that it was not me that was fraught with contradiction, it was society itself. Instead of internalizing my 'failure' I began to be angry, for the first time in my life.

2

1 Thirty eight/thirty nine years: more holiday snaps. But not on beaches. I seem to have placed myself, each time, in such a way as to signify that I am now a 'tourist'.

These 'exotic' backgrounds mask my own total lack of

knowledge of the social and economic conditions of these countries, through which I was briefly 'packaged'.

But then I don't own any land or buildings in front of which to be photographed.

The colour prints were

made at Grunwicks. (*David Phillips, deceased/writer, friend and lover*)

2 Forty years: taken against the light, this Easy Rider image, with its hippy connotations, pleased me. It broke right through my

own image of middle age. I will always treasure it, not only for what it didn't show of me (!) but because it was taken by someone who helped me through a rough period of my life, as did his family. (*Martin Head/photographer/ friend*)

THESE three portraits were all taken for totally different reasons.

1   This was taken by my boyfriend when we were just getting to know each other. I was making an effort to look 'feminine' at the time, curling my hair, wearing earrings, bright colours. I felt good.

I felt poised when it was taken, trying at the same time to look pensive yet affectionate.

It was taken with a large format camera, using the Zone System of exposure control in order to lose skin detail and render the surface white and smooth, yet still retain good tonal detail and deep blacks elsewhere.
(*Terry Dennett/Photography Workshop*)

2   I asked the photographer to take this for me. He used a large, diffused light source – to simulate north light. I wanted to look serious and unfussy. I would be quite happy if this were the only picture to represent me historically, even though it gives very little clue beyond the signs present on the face, emphasized through the use of a particular visual rhetoric.
(*Ed Barber/photographer*)

3   This medical record of me was made five days after I had blown myself up with the gas stove whilst cooking dinner. Wearing my glasses had saved my eyes from damage, but my face was badly singed, my front hair burnt off and my eyebrows mostly missing.

The picture was taken with flat, bounced, lighting in order to record detail. I tried to be devoid of an emotive (pathetic) expression, but wanted to clearly register my shocked condition.
(*Terry Dennett*)

Each of these three pictures has its own field of meanings. For instance they could be read as expressions of my 'womanliness', or my 'intelligence', or my 'stupidity'. I would hardly give photograph 3 to a lover as a keepsake. I could be seen as in control of the situation, or not. What social class am I from in these various pictures?

How does this affect the meanings if you don't know anything about me? What value judgements will you start making because I'm not very pretty, or wear these sort of glasses, or don't show my tits? Suppose you had only seen one of them?

In our culture the face is supposedly the repository of our character or our personality. It is used to represent us, and photographed constantly. Quite clearly *how* it is photographed and by whom is a matter for some concern. Quite clearly also *it cannot possibly represent us*, even though we are taught that it can. We must learn to see beyond ourselves and the stereotypes offered, to understand the invisible class and power relationships into which we are structured from birth.

We must begin to question photographs, asking not only what we think they show us (and how much of what we think we perceive is in fact based on the particular type of visual rhetoric worked upon the sitter), but also what they don't (can't?) show us.

3

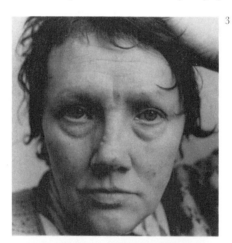

2

1

TAKING more control: of myself, as well as of what goes on in front of the camera. These are all 'fictions' of me – as are all photographs. Each shows different ways of 'seeing' myself.

I have never liked anything about the way I look. Each particular part of me was 'wrong'. Trying to 'improve' upon things was somehow cheating. People should have to work to find out what goes on under the surface. (By 'people', of course, I meant men.)

There must be a way to reconcile the contradiction of living with a face and body you don't really like. I have only ever been bits and pieces, symptoms and faults. Never an organic whole. Who could I blame for this? Of course, myself.

What rubbish . . . how could I be to blame? The whole thing is a fiction.

I am what I *do*.

I am also what I don't do.

Food, beauty, love, health, sexuality, clothing, free time . . . all have become commodities now

removed from actual bodily 'needs'. How do I know what my needs are? My body (which is the centre of the battlefield) should become an area where sexuality, health, leisure and labour can become integrated. When they are integrated the energy can be channelled with the anger; the anger with the consciousness.

But first I have to look at the various fragments; symbolically put them together again. I have to reclaim myself.

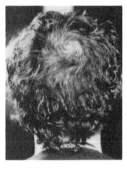

9

PUBLIC IMAGES

1 How I'd like to look.

2 How others see me – their descriptions surround me.

3 What happens when you completely change one part of your face?

4 Or add a moustache?

5 Wiping out my old face with grease paint.

6 Dressing up. Being made up by somebody else is very sensual. I was not allowed to look at myself

until I was finished. My 'tartiness' upset me initially.

7 Self consciousness vanished in this supportive atmosphere. This was a session of the Faces Group in 1976.

8 Mark II tart. This picture is not about my sexuality, but is about my visually bantering with a particular stereotype. This open flaunting of surface sexuality released pent up anger about various things I had suppressed in myself.

Only by allowing others whom I trusted to take over my face and body could I break through the image of how I *thought* I looked. It made it possible to go back to my 'everyday' face secure in the knowledge that I *could* look different – but I no longer wanted to.

9 The day my hair fell out – after a visit to the hairdressers. I made a special point of having it photographed.

1

How do we invent our lives out of a limited range of possibilities, and how are our lives invented for us by those in power?
Sekula

2

3

HOW can we begin to change the portrait, to change ideas of what should and should not go into our family albums?

I like these 'progressive' and 'realistic' pictures of myself, (although I realize that they are not something 'pure' which I can hang on to – advertising could easily adopt any of them to make sales for aspirins, face cream, or drugs). They do give an indication though of how much information about us is lacking from this 'private' context.

These pictures were all taken in the 'documentary' mode. This means that room lighting was used, I was not specially posed, and they try to give an indication of what actually 'happened'. This is very different from a traditional portrait which is usually specially lit, posed and decontextualized.

1 Portrait by a feminist friend, in conversation. (*Michael Anne Mullen/ photographer/friend*)

2 Late night. (*Terry Dennett/Photography Workshop*)

3 Early Morning. (*Terry Dennett*)

4 Hayfever on washing day. (*Terry Dennett*)

Many people have remarked how brave I was to be photographed in this way. The 'late night' picture (top right) appeared on the cover of *Spare Rib* magazine. Is it brave? Why? Nobody ever came up to me in the street and said I was brave to walk around like that.

4

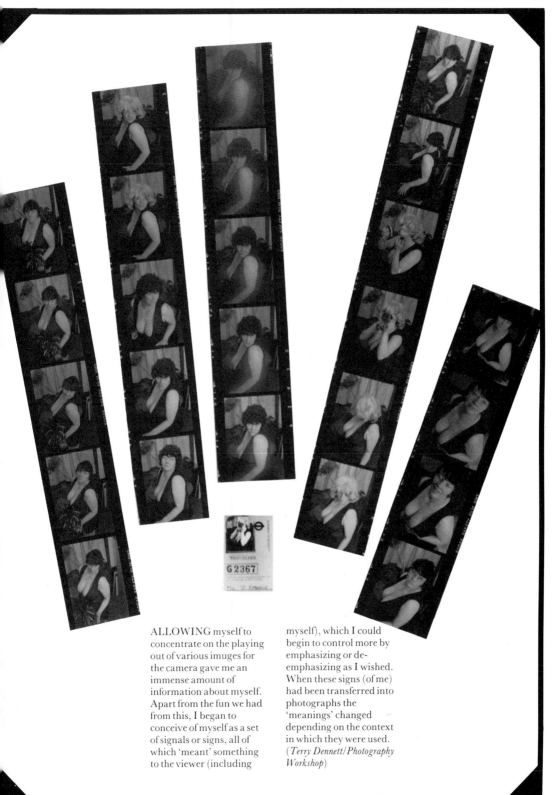

ALLOWING myself to concentrate on the playing out of various imuges for the camera gave me an immense amount of information about myself. Apart from the fun we had from this, I began to conceive of myself as a set of signals or signs, all of which 'meant' something to the viewer (including myself), which I could begin to control more by emphasizing or de-emphasizing as I wished. When these signs (of me) had been transferred into photographs the 'meanings' changed depending on the context in which they were used. (*Terry Dennett/Photography Workshop*)

as he kissed her, Snow White awoke.

Women are at their best slaving over a hot stove.

We've come a long, long way.

VIRGINIA SLIMS

At last, a cigarette we can call our own.

EVERY PACKET CARRIES A GOVERNMENT HEALTH WARNING.

The new Body Language bra.
Because the bust you've always wanted is probably your own

Body Language bra

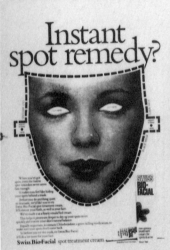

Instant spot remedy?

Swiss Bio-Facial spot treatment cream

Start as you mean to go on.

HEAL'S

The Love Department

paul

The Love Department
Paul planned it around the Moffat-Fiesta

FOR TODAY'S PARENTS

mother   March 1978   35p

Facts and Fables about BREAST-FEEDING

DON'T LOVE MY CHILD

DRUGS or DISCIPLINE A STARTLING CLAIM

MAKE A GAME OF LEARNING TO READ

"It rained. I broke the teapot. I missed the shops."

but he has a way of making things turn out fine.

Now she can cope.

Stelazine
the one to turn to.

SK&F

TIMES of great changes. Friendships now based on mutual interests, similar class experience. Living with differing political beliefs, differing gender socialization . . . with more flexibility. But increasing anger.

This period is too close to write about autobiographically. I began to like women though. They no longer seemed just people to fill up time with until the right man came along. But it's too late to be my mother's friend.

I am not a mother. Nor do I want to be one. I am willing to help to take social responsibility for myself and others, but I am not willing to undergo the trauma of individualized misery and sacrifice that 'motherhood' means in our culture.

Those who are parents and manage to stay integrated, bring up their children, and continue to struggle against the rigid gender, race and class positions assigned to them have my utmost respect. Any work I do in the future will revolve around ways of understanding, and articulating, this struggle between parents and children; between families and the wider social and economic spheres; between ideology and actuality; between classes.

My continual rethinking of the past, as my consciousness changes, is impossible to stabilize.

This reworking is initially painful, confusing, extreme. As I become more aware of how I have been constructed ideologically, as the *method* becomes clearer, there is no peeling away of layers to reveal a 'real' self, just a constant reworking process. I realize that I am a process.

These pictures are here for no better reason than they remind me of happy times and of people I love.

FAIRY TALES AND PHOTOGRAPHY
1980

Much further work came out of *Beyond the Family Album*, in particular, work concerned with representing the unrepresentable.

Psychoanalysis has theorized that unless we can consciously represent something to ourselves we are unable to speak about it and thereby change it. So much in my family photographs had been mythologized and so much was missing, and so much of my memory was off-limits that it became almost impossible to conceptualize my own past beyond a series of anecdotes related to me by parents and grandparents. Turning to various histories of the class into which I was born, later to feminist histories, and then to histories of the state and of institutions (particularly of schooling and medicine) I began to grasp a wider problem for me as a photographer and social historian: how could I represent the power structures in which we are formed as children, and which then pin us in place? A picture of me as a schoolgirl says little about the social relations or politics of education, nor does it give any indication of my subjective experience of educational institutions.

From this period came the desire to document my own family life differently (we were in the middle of a family divorce, which is like trying to photograph a war). The problem was that of trying to 'speak visually' about what we see going on around us, and what happens to us. My brother's family split-up was so acrimonious and distressing to everybody that I floundered about in trying to represent it. Although I took hundreds of pictures, which are now in our family archive, I was only able to use a few for public display and then had to write the text as a series of equations which posed questions, rather than a series of statements. I was already beginning to understand that we should use photos to ask questions rather than to try to show facts.

From 1980 to 1982, whilst a student at the Polytechnic of Central London, I made an extensive study of the evolution of the Cinderella story, looking particularly at the pictures which had hardly changed at all in over a hundred years, consisting of roughly twelve or less different tableaux. I came to the conclusion that the many possible meanings of the story were limited to very

Family album as fairy story

few possibilities by the specificity of these pictures. In most stories the pictures repeat what the words tell us, so I began to be interested in pictures which by saying something different from the text opened up a space for new meanings to emerge. I wanted to contradict or demythologize the story.

I therefore created and illustrated my own version of the tale, using images of my brother and two nieces as a one-parent family and incorporating events in their lives. This was not a simple posing of the 'fantasy' of the story against the 'reality' of their lives, but an interweaving of elements with different status, so that I could pose new questions about the people who inhabited Cinderella, and the people who inhabit the social and psychic world of everyday life.

Cinderella

As though to punish the girl further, the stepsisters were given the finest clothes to wear, and the most luxurious rooms to sleep in, while the poor child had just one dull dress, and was forced to sleep in a cold attic room on a mattress of straw. Her only comfort was to rest each evening, in the chimney corner, among the ashes and cinders of the fire. And because of this they called her Cinderella. But despite her dusty, ragged clothes, Cinderella was very beautiful, a hundred times more beautiful than her stepsisters in all their finery.

Now it happened one day, that the King's son was giving a ball to which all the fashionable people in the kingdom were invited, and Cinderella's stepsisters were, of course, included. They were most excited and could talk of nothing but the ball, and the clothes they would wear. For Cinderella this meant more work than ever. She had to wash all her sisters' clothes, just in case they might choose this dress or that petticoat.

Once upon a time there was a young girl whose mother died and left her to be brought up by her father. She was a pretty, kind-hearted girl, and she had promised her mother, before she died, that she would always try to be good. So the girl and her father lived quite happily together, until the time when he married again. For his second wife, he chose a proud and spiteful woman. She also had two ugly daughters, and they were equally cruel and bad-tempered. With the three of them, the poor young girl knew not a minute's peace.

They bullied and teased her from morning till night, making her wait on them, and do all the worst jobs in the house. She swept their rooms, washed the dishes, scrubbed the floors and never complained, for she remembered her promise to be good. But this made her stepmother even more envious. The young girl's pretty looks and sweet nature made her stepsisters appear more ugly and disagreeable than ever.

They called for her and shouted at her all day long:

'Cinderella! You must help me to decide what to wear.'

'Cinderella! My hair needs brushing.'

'Cinderella! Come here this minute. I want you to do my make-up.'

'Cinderella! Cinderella!'

The poor child was run off her feet, but she accepted all this extra work without complaint, and did her best to make her stepsisters look as fine as possible.

While they chattered away, and sat admiring themselves in their grand mirrors, Cinderella was working hard. Then one sister said, 'Cinderella, wouldn't you like to be going to the ball?'

'Oh, very much,' said Cinderella. But then she saw how they grinned, and she said, 'But you are teasing me. How could I go to such a grand ball?'

'How indeed!' the sisters sneered. 'Just think how everyone would stare if they saw a cinder-wench like you dancing.' And they laughed and laughed and laughed.

Soon it was time to leave. Cinderella watched her stepsisters drive away in a fine carriage, and at last her own unhappiness was too much to bear. She sat in her place by the fire, and began to cry.

Now Cinderella had one good friend, her godmother, and just then she chanced to call. Her godmother asked why she was crying. Cinderella tried to tell her, 'I wish . . . Oh, how I wish . . .' But she couldn't speak for her tears.

'You wish you could go to the ball, don't you?' said her wise godmother.

'Yes, more than anything in the world,' answered Cinderella.

'And so you shall,' said her godmother. 'Let us see what we can do. The first problem is how to get you there.'

She led Cinderella into the garden and sent her to find a pumpkin. Cinderella couldn't see how a pumpkin would help, but she did as she was told. Now, Cinderella's godmother was a fairy, and when she took the pumpkin she lightly touched it with her wand. The pumpkin swelled and swelled, until it grew into an elegant coach, which shone like gold. Next she went to the mouse-trap where she found six live mice.

She told Cinderella to lift the trap-door carefully, and, as each mouse ran out, she quickly tapped it with her wand. Instantly the mice turned into six fine grey horses to lead the wonderful coach. Now they needed a coachman. Cinderella went to the rat-trap. Inside was a small rat which she took to her godmother. One touch of her wand changed him into a smart coachman, dressed in livery, ready to drive the coach. Finally, Cinderella was sent to find six lizards. With a little more magic, they became six splendid footmen to ride with the coach and wait on Cinderella. She was going to travel to the ball in fine style!

'There now,' said her godmother, 'this is fit for a princess. Are you ready to go?'
'Oh, yes indeed,' said Cinderella, 'but what about my ragged dress?' Just one more touch of the wand, and at once her rags became a magnificent gown of shining satin, and on her feet were a pair of extraordinary slippers made of pure gold, in which she could dance like a fairy.

At last she was completely ready. Cinderella stepped into the coach feeling like a true princess. But before she left, her godmother warned, 'You must be home before midnight! The magic will not last a moment longer. When the clock strikes twelve, the coach will become a pumpkin, the horses mice, the coachman a rat, the footmen lizards, and your lovely clothes will turn into rags once more.' Cinderella promised to be home in time and, completely happy, she set off for the ball.

When she arrived at the palace she was introduced as a princess, and the King's son came to greet her. As he led Cinderella into the hall everyone stopped dancing, even the music stopped. The whole company stood back to admire this unknown princess. She looked so beautiful that everyone was amazed, and when she danced she charmed them even more. The Prince would dance with no one else, and sat beside her throughout the evening. There was a marvellous supper served but the Prince ate nothing; he could only gaze at Cinderella. During supper, Cinderella sat beside her stepsisters and talked with them about all manner of things, but they did not recognise her. They were flattered that the beautiful princess sat with them, never suspecting who she might be.

After supper the Prince again danced with Cinderella and paid her many compliments. She was so happy that she completely forgot the time.

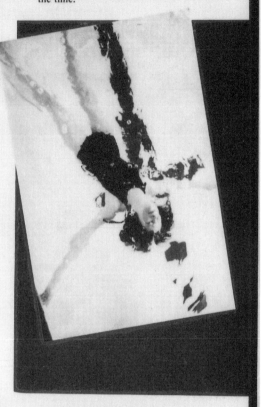

Suddenly the clock began to strike twelve: One! Two! Three! In panic Cinderella fled from the hall.
Four! Five! Six! She ran down the great staircase, never daring to look back. On the way she lost one of her gold slippers but there was no time to stop.
Seven! Eight! Nine! Away she ran, across the courtyard. She could hear voices now, and the sound of footsteps behind her, but she didn't look back.
Ten! Eleven! Twelve! And she was gone. By the time she left the palace grounds she was dressed once more in rags; all the magic had vanished. All except one of her little gold slippers, which she clutched in her hand.

27

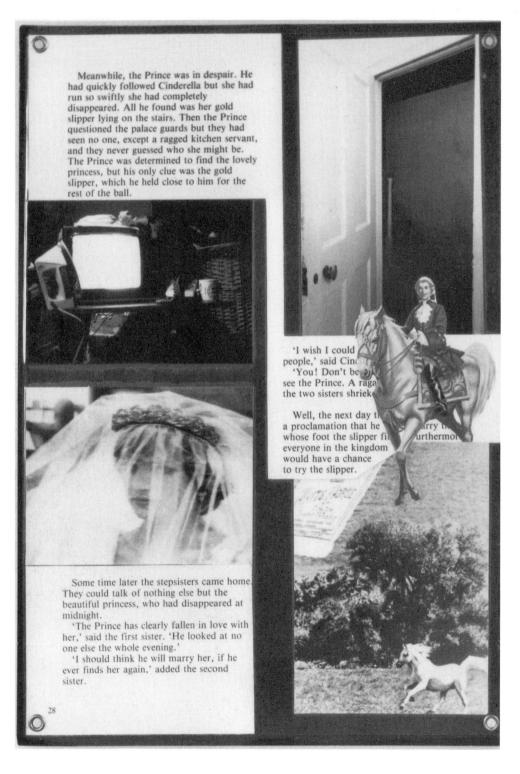

Meanwhile, the Prince was in despair. He had quickly followed Cinderella but she had run so swiftly she had completely disappeared. All he found was her gold slipper lying on the stairs. Then the Prince questioned the palace guards but they had seen no one, except a ragged kitchen servant, and they never guessed who she might be. The Prince was determined to find the lovely princess, but his only clue was the gold slipper, which he held close to him for the rest of the ball.

'I wish I could people,' said Cind
'You! Don't be see the Prince. A raga the two sisters shriek

Well, the next day a proclamation that he whose foot the slipper fi everyone in the kingdom would have a chance to try the slipper.

Some time later the stepsisters came home They could talk of nothing else but the beautiful princess, who had disappeared at midnight.

'The Prince has clearly fallen in love with her,' said the first sister. 'He looked at no one else the whole evening.'

'I should think he will marry her, if he ever finds her again,' added the second sister.

28

First of all, the princesses tried, and then the duchesses, and after that, all the ladies of the court, but of course it was all in vain. There was only one person in the world whom this slipper would fit.

At last the slipper was brought for the two stepsisters to try. Each sister in turn tried to force her clumsy foot into the dainty slipper. They pushed and pulled and tugged, until they were red in the face, but without success. Then the Prince asked, 'Are there no other young ladies here?' Cinderella, who had watched secretly from the kitchen, stepped forward and asked if she might try. Her stepsisters burst out laughing, and said, 'Certainly not!'

But the Prince silenced them. 'Everyone must try the slipper,' he said, and he turned to Cinderella, 'Please sit down.'

Of course the slipper slid onto her foot easily, and she took the matching slipper from her pocket. Thereupon her godmother appeared, and once more transformed Cinderella's clothes into a fine gown. Then the Prince and everyone else recognised her as the beautiful princess. At this her stepsisters were amazed. They begged Cinderella to forgive them, and tried to excuse their wickedness towards her. In her goodness, Cinderella embraced them both, and said, 'From now on we must love each other as true sisters.'

Soon after, the Prince and Cinderella were married. The wedding was a grand affair and Cinderella's stepsisters were invited. They were introduced to two great lords of the court and in time they also were married. Thanks to Cinderella, who was as good as she was beautiful, everyone lived happily ever after.

WORKING FOR THE MEDIA ... OR MAKING THE MEDIA WORK FOR US 1979 ONWARDS

In 1979, at the time of the Hayward Gallery exhibition, I was at the height of my naivety. I had already been involved in different ventures within alternative publishing and had even helped to set up the magazine *Camerawork* with Terry Dennett and others, and was fairly disillusioned with the process. In addition, I had not understood that work like mine and the Hackney Flashers, in entering the 'art' arena, would be subjected to entirely different criteria from those of community photography, left-wing or women's movement circles. It was a salutary exercise to find it written off as mere 'therapy' (my work), or 'fit to hang in church halls' (Hackney Flashers). When I was approached by Carol Bell from the BBC's *Arena* programme to discuss some of the issues raised in the exhibition, I felt dubious about how to represent myself on television. I felt equally anxious about how to indicate that the ideas I was trying to represent were not 'mine' but came from a particular position within debates on oral history and visual representation. In the event Carol Bell did a magnificent job, and the resultant twenty minute programme has been useful for a variety of purposes since it was transmitted.

I feel in retrospect that I was lulled into a state of over-confidence, for several years later when I was approached by the BBC's *Omnibus* team, I readily agreed to take part in a programme on photographic style. I documented the resultant fiasco (of what I can only call misrepresentation) in January 1983 in an article in *Screen*. In essence, the director of the programme offered an adequate amount of time to demonstrate and 'state my case', which was then hacked to pieces in the cutting room and the flow of my argument totally disrupted and diminished. I now gather that this is a regular part of television's working practice, but at the time I was inexperienced enough to think that I could work against the grain in a programme which offered yet another privileging of photography as fine art in the guise of a study of style.

Since then I have had intermittent brushes with various television companies, some of which used me quite sensibly, whilst others blatantly misled me about the space on offer to me in any given programme. An example was my inclusion in a programme

on Cinderella in 1966. I had amassed an enormous archive of Cinderella ephemera but in spite of my being assured that I could cover the points I wanted, in the end it was the archive itself which was privileged. I felt I looked like a Cinderella-groupie. My relevant work as a wedding photographer and photo therapist was also glossed over.

This experience finally convinced me that if I wanted to be useful to cultural debates I should attempt to use television in a totally different way by making my own proposals direct to companies. To this end, Nina Kellgren, Moya Burns and I have made proposals, via the production company Large Door, to Channel Four Television for a series of educational programmes on amateur photography.

To be fodder for the fantasies of other cultural workers no longer appeals to me, though I still feel that it is possible to work against the flow of television by presenting ideas in a non-naturalistic way, and have been influenced to this end by the French film director Godard and Fassbinder's contributions to German television. However, it remains to be seen whether or not Nina, Moya and I can achieve our objectives in the way we hope.

Early attempts at ironically juxtaposing images from different discourses led to my producing a 'passport' of my history. This was a book which I could give to a total stranger to explain how I felt about myself and the world. It was a technique taught me by Keith Kennedy, an arts teacher.

In the late 1970s, women questioned their perceptions of themselves in a range of workshop situations. Here, in The Faces group, Lyn is confronted with several different masks of her face made from photographs I had taken. Using make up and dressing up in old clothes was another way of breaking down and moving through the stereotyped images offered us by the media. The work was quite frightening to some of us, and never moved far beyond the face as the place we admitted to disliking. Had we but known it, what we were articulating was a form of self hatred, now dealt with more easily in assertiveness training and in women's therapy groups.

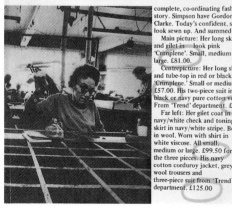

PHOTOGRAPHY/ POLITICS:ONE

complete, co-ordinating fashion story. Simpson have Gordon Clarke. Today's confident, stylish look sewn up. And summed up.
Main picture: Her long skirt and gilet in   look pink 'Crimplene'. Small, medium or large. £81.00.
Centrepicture: Her long skirt and tube-top in red or black 'Crimplene.' Small or medium. £57.00. His two-piece suit in black or navy pure cotton velvet. From 'Trend' department. £95.00
Far left: Her gilet coat in navy/white check and toning skirt in navy/white stripe. Both in wool. Worn with shirt in white viscose. All small, medium or large. £99.50 for the three pieces. His navy cotton corduroy jacket, grey wool trousers and three-piece suit from 'Trend' department. £125.00

Photography Workshop's first major publication in 1979, Photography/ Politics: One, *edited by Terry Dennett, David Evans, Sylvia Gohl and myself, was funded in part by my severance pay for my expulsion from the* Camerawork *collective, in part by forward subscriptions, in part from our own earnings. Self-publishing might be seen as an exciting venture from the outside, but from the inside it was sheer bloody hard work. When the printer delivered the first batch of 2,000 we could hardly move in our home for books everywhere. The first edition sold out quickly and was reprinted from sales of the first. We did not generate enough capital to produce the second volume, which was done by a commercial publisher.*

spare Rib

35 pence
issue 68 march 78
a women's liberation magazine

"This is now one of my
favourite pictures"

A photographer looks at herself

Houston, Texas – the Women's Moderation Movement?
Fleet Street straightens out lesbian mothers
Hairdressing juniors – the bald facts
Understanding cervical smears
What's up on Tyneside
My day at the S.S.

Many women photographers support Spare Rib. *My 'realistic' portrait on their cover in 1978 caused a few shock waves, and I delighted to see it on sale alongside more orthodox magazines with their blandly smiling models.*

The photo story came out of Spare Rib's *desire to have a 'visual' issue. After several meetings with their editorial staff we women photographers went off singly and in groups to produce our contribution. The office scenes were shot at the British Film Institute where I worked and the bedroom scenes in the home of a secretary with whom I worked.*

NO 163 ● FEBRUARY 1986 ● 80p

SPARE *Rib*

A WOMEN'S LIBERATION MAGAZINE

C A N C E R

E X P O S U R

▲ **gertrude shope on revolution in south africa**

● **life in death-trap divis, belfast**

■ **denise black and the kray sisters**

I again appeared on the cover of Spare Rib in 1986 in connection with my article 'The Picture of Health'. The picture of me was taken by Rosy Martin during a photo therapy session (more of which later) on powerlessness. The years between these two covers show the major shift in my own thinking about reality and fantasy. What is the relationship between the two, and how does it relate to visual imagery?

Part of my contribution to the BBC's Omnibus *programme in 1982 on photographic styles was an attempt to indicate that two photographs taken by cameras sitting side by side could be used in different ways.*

Add a little VO5 Conditioner to your life and you can expect a lot more.

Go for the one that suits you best. From new Camomile to Henna, there are six different VO5 types. One for every type of hair.

Every one has more going for you. With more shine and more body. To make you look and feel great. After all, VO5 outshines the others. And so will you.

Alberto VO5 Conditioners. The Outshiners.

More Shine. More Body.

Is this what you struggled to get your 'A' levels for?

Cussons
(U.K.) LTD

Registered No. 748096 England.

FINE SOAPS AND BATH LUXURIES

REGISTERED OFFICE **K E R S A L   V A L E**
M A N C H E S T E R   M7 OGL
PHONE   061-792 6111

GRAMS   KERVALLI, MANCHESTER, 7
TELEX   669803

YOUR REF   OUR REF

KAS/MR

15th November, 1982

B.B.C. T.V.,
Shepherds Bush,
London, W.12.

Dear Sirs,

As manufacturers of Morning Fresh Washing Up Liquid, we would be
interested to learn if prints of the photographs taken by Jo Spence
could be made available to us. These were of the model Jilly Johnson
and shown during your Omnibus programme.

Yours faithfully,
CUSSONS (U.K.) LTD.

10.40* Omnibus

with Barry Norman
Lord Lichfield, Jane Bown (*Observer*), Beverley Goodway (*Sun*), educational and feminist photographer **Jo Spence** and surrealist **Bob Carlos Clarke** were challenged to photograph top model **Jilly Johnson** in whatever style they thought appropriate.
A Week in the Country: **John Morley**, modern pre-Raphaelite, painter of nature and still life, lived in Suffolk when director **John Read** met him at work in the days before his first London exhibition.
Film cameraman COLIN WALDECK
Film editor JULIAN MILLER
Photography producer BERNARD CLARK
Film cameraman BRIAN HALL
Editor CHRISTOPHER MARTIN

■ Omnibus 10.40-11.30 BBC1.
Jilly Johnson made a name for herself as a 'Page Three bird.' Now's your chance to see the facts behind the figure and the face behind the lens in this 'Omnibus' which purports to demystify glamour photography. The recipe is good enough: take five famous photographers and ask them to explain how different photographic styles/techniques affect the presentation of the subject matter. So, Patrick Lichfield, Jane Bown and token politico, Jo Spence, line up their shutters on the delightful Jilly. The audience is treated to half an hour of non stop titillation and voyeuristic delights as Jilly bounces, pouts and poses. Hot stuff, and any attempt made by Jo Spence to suggest that there's more to a camera than meets the eye are cut short. As a consequence any potentially critical comment on the problems of photographing female flesh are sent to the wall. Objectification, exploitation, commodity fetishism... never heard of it.
　In the second part of the programme, John Read talks to modern Pre-Raphaelite painter, John Morley.

I had one fan letter – from Cussons!

Making Omnibus with the BBC. Programme previews from Radio Times *and* City Limits.

Part of a proposal made to Channel Four Television in 1986 by myself, Nina Kellgren and Moya Burns to make five programmes about amateur photography. These are from the programme on holiday snaps and tourism.

Emboldened by the heady atmosphere of the journey I offered to go into the lion's den. Everyone watches, cameras at the ready . . .

We can pay to dress up as mythical heroes in order to be photographed (jokingly) for the family album. The boy who looks after the camels watches with cynicism.

At the hotel I buy a postcard to send home. As I go back to my room I notice a tiny cupboard on the landing. Later, I realize that our room maid lives there. Such is the essence of what we are encouraged to 'see' and 'notice'.

L ANDSCAPE PHOTOGRAPHY 1979

I spent a pleasurable weekend at a Paul Hill Workshop in Newcastle, and my attempts at landscape photography (riven through with my sense of humour) convinced me to forget about it. . .

R EMODELLING PHOTO HISTORY
1981 TO 1982

At this period, Terry Dennett and I attempted to look closely and clearly at the way photography works in our society. The article, which we wrote at the time, explains what our project was about. The photos which follow show the work in practice.

REMODELLING PHOTO HISTORY:
A Collaboration Between Two Photographers

Terry Dennett and Jo Spence

For those of us who are photographic workers it is obvious that a vast amount of work still needs to be done on the so-called history of photography, and on the practices, institutions and apparatuses of photography itself, and the function they have had in constructing and encouraging particular ways of viewing and telling about the world. The photo work which follows is an exploration of our attempts to work through some of this problem by 'making strange' the everyday, normalized, institutional practices and codes of 'the trade', re-ordered, re-modelled, re-invented, so that their commonsense, unquestioned notions become disrupted. We are not trying to show familiar objects in unfamiliar ways, but rather to denaturalize the genres of photography which already consist of fully coded visual signs. Much of our thinking on this has been influenced by reading and seeing the work of Brecht, and by the writings of Augusto Boal.

This piece of work is a very tiny statement which should be seen in the tradition of 'worker photography' – our workplace being photography as a production process in which we are daily involved. As two working photographers, we have tried any number of ways of making and using photographs so that they do not merely parrot the dominant modes of visual representations of the left, centre, or right of cultural practices and politics but call such practices into question so that it begins to be easier to understand that the camera is not a window on the world, nor are meanings of pictures fixed, but that visual signs (in this case photographs) are in themselves sites of struggle. In trying to make a piece of work 'about' photography, we are making a break with our former work, but as life-long photographers we feel it might be useful to look at the ways in which various institutions and

apparatuses have used and validated photography, and to try, within that perspective, to make a visual/verbal statement on work and sexuality.

The highest product of capitalism (*after John Heartfield***).**

Above all, we wanted to get away from the dry didacticism which pervades so much worthy work on photographic theory and to provide instead a kind of 'revolt' from within the ranks. In a funny sort of way this is a return to our class roots, where adversity and oppression are dealt with not only through comradely struggles or learned exposition, but lived out through individual or group rituals like sarcasm or irony (what is commonly termed 'taking the piss'). We aimed to produce something which was perhaps not quite in such 'good taste' as is usually expected; something which tried to break down some of the sacred cows of photography and bourgeois aesthetics while daring to mention police photography and fashion photography in the very same breath, to indicate that perhaps they share some common formal features.

What we finally hit upon was a form of photo-theatre. Here we could use non-naturalistic modes of representation which allowed us to create a kind of hybrid 'spectacle' whilst drawing upon and disrupting well-known genres of photography which have been concerned with the representation of aspects of the female body. Obviously this collaboration between two photographers, using themselves both as photographer and as photographic object, stems from our joint interests in photography and politics. So whilst attempting to engage with some of the current theories of visual representation, we are at the same time attempting to offer a critique of standard histories of photography, which still mostly exclude details of institutional, state, class or economic determinants, being grounded rather in 'great inventions', 'great names', 'great companies' and 'great themes'. The work particularly allowed us to draw upon our separate experiences as a scientific photographer and photo historian (Terry) and as an ex-commercial and ex-portrait photographer now working on the visual/socio-economic history of the family (Jo).

We decided not to rely on what we could find to photograph (in the classic documentary sense), nor on montaging visual elements at the post-shooting stage, nor on 'subversive' texts. We wanted to provide a twin performance – the staging and acting out of a tableau for the camera, done by us as social actor/s, and then a two dimensional signifying performance on film and paper. Within this framework we had extended discussions in order to pre-visualize and script everything but still leave room for an element of spontaneity at the shooting stage. We did this work sporadically across several months, taking long weekends to drive around looking for props and locations, and to do the actual shooting. Working mostly with large format cameras on tripods, we could economically re-shoot anything we were not entirely satisfied with. Drawing upon our long disused but internalized professional experience, we chose how to depict a range of styles and genres, both contemporary and historical. By adding a sparse text (what amounted to a recategorization process), we hoped the spectator could make new inferences.

Crucial to this project was the fact that we wanted to re-examine and re-work the model/photographer relationship, which is generally so one-sided. At the same time as we drew upon our own knowledge of the codes and signifying practices of portraiture, record, still life, documentary, fashion and 'nude' photography, we also traversed what we knew of photo practices from within fine art, anthropology, news, advertising, science, law, medicine, welfare and charity institutions. We did not attempt the futile task of trying to invent another language, but tried rather to indicate how photographs which are usually given a currency and circulated within different (and apparently contradictory) spheres can, when brought together in this disruptive way, enable the viewer to make new and political connections.

Although *Remodelling Photo History* attempts to map out relationships between the apparatuses which use and straddle photography and the institutions which validate or teach photographic practices, we also wanted to indicate how this linked up with the placing of women within the family by showing that there is consistency between some of the ways in which oppressed women and other subordinated groups are represented. Though the project offers a starting point from within photography, it allows us to move beyond the eternal textual analysis to ask questions about what is not being shown or said; what cannot be said (what is visually unsayable); and what is being displaced or rendered structurally absent. In asking what is absent we enter the realm of the analytical, be it through psychoanalysis or historical materialism. The former engages with the construction of our gendered subjectivity, unconscious desires and pleasures, positioned as we are within familial relationships and within texts in specific discourses; the latter engages with the possibility of conscious scientific and socially useful historical knowledge and the possibility of political change. Both realms address memory – that which is considered unthinkable/unspeakable/unknowable, socially censored from consciousness, and that which in terms of class/power relations is rendered invisible, not named/discussed/shown and often actively suppressed.

Apart from hoping to give some critical pleasure to an audience, part of our project has been to find a pleasurable new way of working together. Previous collaborations between us have revolved around notions of photography for social and political action, and we wanted to do something which would allow us to explore our personal as well as our working lives and political relationships. Finally we wanted to pose questions beyond the scope of these images. Since we'd been working within a Brechtian tradition of distanciation, trying to transform feeling into thinking and questioning through a form of 'educational entertainment', we turned to Brecht's own writing. His questioning poem, coming from outside photographic discourse, seemed relevant to the overall problems of history – both of the individual gendered subject, and to our positioning within a hierarchical class society.

(Incidentally, what we can't or don't ask of most photographs is questions of *their* history. . .)

Excerpts from an article first published in SCREEN, vol. 23, no. 1, 1982.

Industrialization

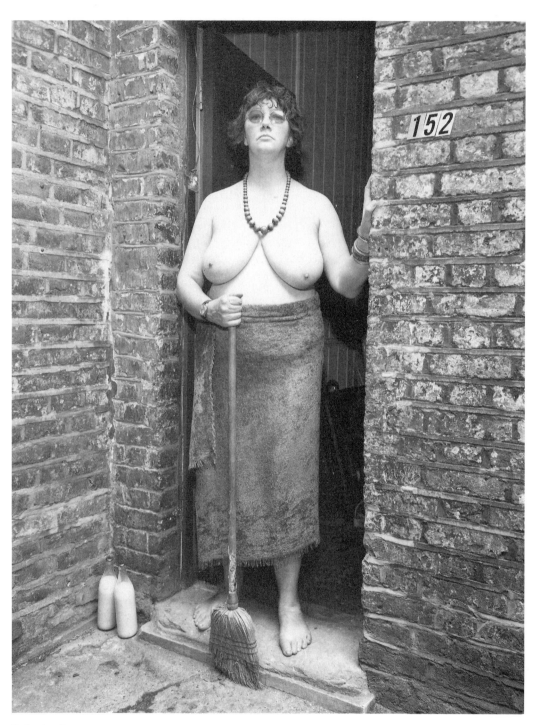

Colonization

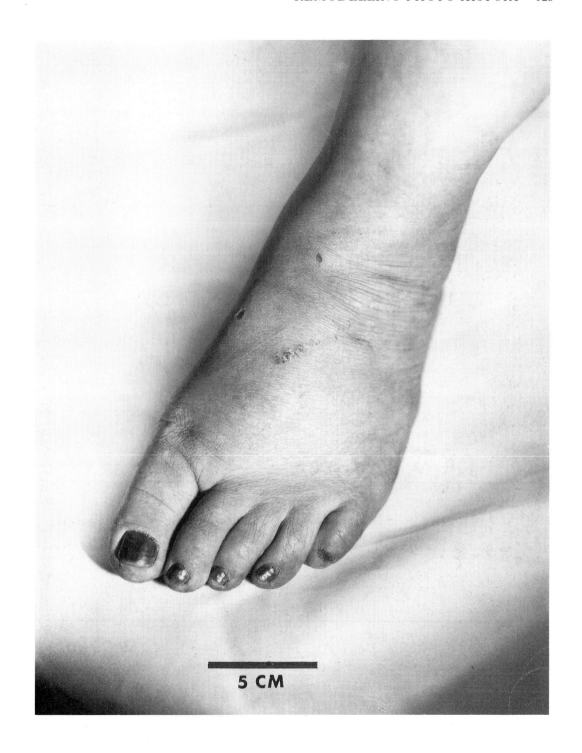

5 CM

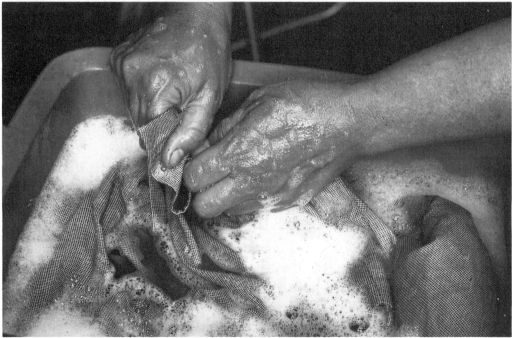

Victimization

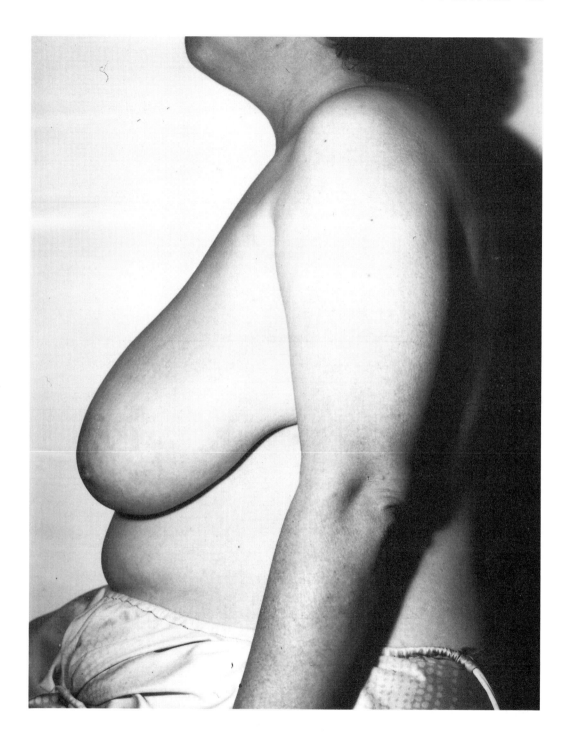

Realization

Revisualization

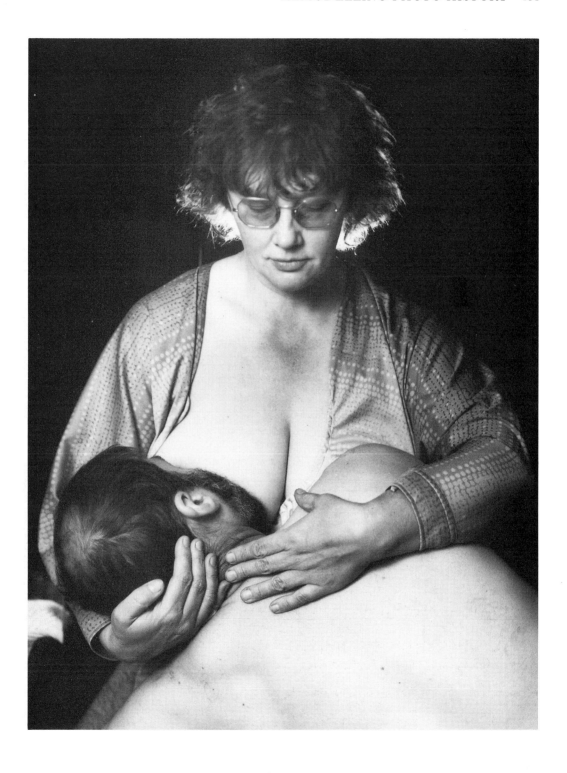

Questions From a Worker Who Reads

Who built Thebes of the seven gates?
In the books you will find the names of kings.
Did the kings haul up the lumps of rock?
And Babylon, many times demolished
Who raised it up so many times? In what houses
Of gold-glittering Lima did the builders live?
Where, the evening that the Wall of China was finished
Did the masons go? Great Rome
Is full of triumphal arches. Who erected them? Over whom
Did the Caesars triumph? Had Byzantium, much praised in song
Only palaces for its inhabitants? Even in fabled Atlantis
The night the ocean engulfed it
The drowning still bawled for their slaves. . .
Every page a victory.
Who cooked the feast for the victors?
Every ten years a great man.
Who paid the bill?

So many reports.
So many questions

Brecht

MATURE STUDENT
1980 TO 1982

By the mid-seventies, my political education was solidly grounded in my belief in working class and women's struggles. My cultural education began in 1976 when I went to work as a secretary for the Education Division of the British Film Institute. In the free-thinking atmosphere of the BFI, I found it stimulating to be typing documents about curriculum innovation and the emerging area of media and film studies, and being centrally involved in cultural debates.

I felt at last that I had something to say and the means with which to say it and the educational chip on my shoulder receded daily as I was encouraged to help set up and run day schools and prepare teaching materials and exhibitions. I researched representations of women in the second world war, grounding academic enquiry within the experience of my own family, and published an article in *Screen* on the representations of white-collar workers in the media – an appropriate field, given that I had spent half my working life as one. I will be eternally grateful to the team I worked with at the BFI.

At the same time, through Photography Workshop, I was lecturing increasingly. None of this was, for me, at all easy. Initially I was very shy, only learning to talk by giving slide lectures alone in darkened rooms. As time passed I gained confidence and, as I got to know my subject matter and stopped worrying about what I didn't know, was able to be open and enthusiastic about the problems of using photography in a range of old and new ways, and to discuss my own limitations in this respect. I have never been ashamed to say that I didn't agree, didn't understand, didn't know, or had changed my mind. I was always interested in revealing how I had worked, as I think that an understanding of process is often more important than the product.

Although my confidence in my views and my power to express them was increasing, by the time of the Hayward exhibition in 1979 I was deep in photographic turmoil. I had moved into a critical position in relation to all the photographic practices I had been involved in, rejecting them as inadequate or politically unethical. I felt I had left myself nowhere to go. Becoming a student seemed a potential way forward and though I lacked a

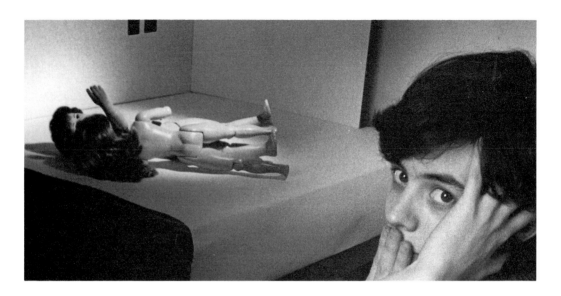

thoretical approach to my subject, empirically I had already arrived at some conclusions I was later to hear academic theoreticians offering back to me. Becoming a student in my forties on the Polytechnic of Central London's photography course was not without its problems.

How can we produce images which foreground contradictions and deal with taboos like incest, so it becomes easier to talk?

At the beginning it was a continual assault on preconceived ideas about what constitutes a photograph, who it is for, what it means, who valued it, who made it, who historicized it. It was also a daily painful experience of feeling inadequate, uncomprehending, unloved, unpolitical, incapable. As students we were on the receiving end of interpenetrating theories of communication, culture, psychoanalysis, semiology, sensitometry, history, feminism, and social and political discourses. We had to learn how to use cameras, film, paper and chemicals, to light and arrange things for the camera, to write up our research and to produce photographs to fulfil specific needs. 'Who are they for?' 'Do the subjects want to be represented that way?' 'Are our images understood?' 'Are they critical enough of the existing social order which daily reproduces itself and in so doing naturalizes that very process of reproduction?' There was no simple 'taking photographs'.

The course was riddled with the contradictions of teaching and learning within a power-based institutional framework. Tutors never ceased to be tutors even if they were political or personal allies. They still occupied positions of power, were still able to close doors on us, to choose not to explain the criteria used in setting up curricula, marking papers or examining pieces of work. Tutors made us very angry for much of the time. They became 'parents' who could never give us enough love and attention, never explain enough, never offer solutions to intractable problems. The relentless drive to get through so much prevented a discussion of how we had been positioned as 'sons' or 'daughters' within authoritarian learning structures. There was never the time to examine the contradictions in discussing the 'Law of the Father' within patriarchy whilst daily subjected to it in the seminar rooms. Only with hindsight can I feel compassion for those unfortunate tutors as they struggled politically within the edifice of higher education to position their courses within a broader map of cultural struggle.

But not all was gloom. I joined with three other students, Mary Ann Kennedy, Jane Munro and Charlotte Pembrey, to produce an exhibition for the degree show. We called ourselves The Polysnappers. Though difficult at first to sink the habits of a lifetime into a continuous collective practice, we shared a political framework and we pooled our knowledge, skills, obsessively-collected image banks and allocations of student materials. Instead of working out who owed who what, we just kept a rough account of who could afford what. It was an ideal situation; for the four of us to spend a major part of eight months on one project would be out of the question under any other conditions. Although we would have found it difficult to minute our discussions and stick to agendas, we became efficient about noting our experiments, filing negatives, handling sensitized materials and working cleanly, all things we felt were an important part of group work.

Because we wanted to produce something which engaged with theoretical issues through familiar material, we centred on the family as a way of making visible all that we as privileged students had learned. We wanted to look at the family as a socially and ideologically produced unit within systems of representation, rather than as a biased or distorted reflection of the real. In Western society, the family, particularly the nuclear family, is seen as the most 'natural' way to live. A lynch pin in our class society, it is often seen as being a universal state, outside of history, outside of power relationships, an ideological haven in the heartless world of capitalism. But though believed to constitute the realm of the 'private', the family is in fact highly public through forms of legislation and taxation, and through institutions of education, welfare and surveillance. Visual representation privileges the nuclear family by naturalizing, romanticizing and idealizing family relationships above all others. We tried to indicate that we could look at the family as an ideological sign system and as a possible site of struggle that could unfix the status quo and promote social change.

Though what we produced can be found in books or dug out of articles we wanted to deal with it photographically so as to make it accessible to a wider audience. We hoped our ways of speaking and picturing could form a bridge back into more abstract concepts.

We used dolls in order to avoid the problems of exploiting as 'camera fodder' those whom we photographed and to enable us to get round the taboo on picturing certain areas of family life. This allowed us to make a greater range of representation than if actual people were used. For example how else could we begin to open up a discussion on pornography within an educational context, or to indicate ways in which mothers are represented as de-eroticized? Additionally, dolls opened up a really pleasurable space for us in which to play. We feel that within a theoretical framework this is important and could be a useful method for initially working through a complexity of ideas. We hope this will be taken up by others in a variety of teaching situations.

By combining dolls with found imagery, we tried to make visible the connection between religion, marriage, myth, advertising and industry. The exhibition, *Family, Fantasy, Photography*, outlived our student lives as we had always intended.

Taking matters into our own hands.

Unclear Family

Most of us live our daily lives in some kind of household or other. And although we all came from 'mummies' and 'daddies' most of us don't spend the rest of our lives living with them (although it is difficult to know how to avoid them as internalized figures of authority.)

People are going into, and coming out of, different types of household or family units throughout their entire lives.

This fact is backed up by the last Census (Office of Population Censuses and Surveys, 'General Household Survey, 1978') which states that only 5% of the population at any one time are actually living in a household consisting of a married couple, with the wife not working, and with two young children.

Yet this is the norm repeatedly propagated and drawn upon in most forms of visual representation.

How do the other 95% live?

How do we ALL get represented?

Panels from the Polysnappers exhibition Family, Fantasy, Photography

1

2

Material Differences

Icons of 'motherhood' are two a penny in our culture – usually narrowed down to the basic oppositional differences of 'good mother' and 'bad mother'. Heroine or victim? – both can be constructed visually from the same subject matter.

Habits of viewing photographs are complex. We carry our 'frames of reference' from our daily experience of life into our interaction with photographs (and all forms of media) – and vice versa. Once we have grasped this, it becomes clear how much power a photographer has when she/he takes as subject matter a living mother and child as a starting point.

The eventual use and context (institutional site) for any photograph will also inform these initial choices. Such choices, usually treated in photographic manuals as 'neutral' – should be thought of rather as ideological building blocks within a wider visual rhetoric. These are not necessarily specific only to photography (though some of them are) but stretch back and across into other forms of art and media.

After we have selected what objects to include, decided on lighting, positioning, angle of view from which to shoot, we still have the choice of whether to work in black and white or in colour materials.

We still have to choose a lens.

We have concentrated here on the use of artificial light in order to have more control, and have used two lenses (a 28mm lens and a 90mm lens) working from exactly the same position in each case.

Crucial shifts of meaning occur when we make the smallest of choices. Sometimes combinations across all these choices can cause such enormous shifts in our perception that we can hardly 'believe our eyes'.

Here the same subject has been treated in the following way:

1 Changing from black and white to colour material (same lens).

2 Changing to a 90mm lens we can now exclude background detail and reduce the picture down to a portrait of the woman and child. Greater transformations occur when we use lighting for 'informational' use, or 'symbolic' use.

3 Changes of lighting convey major changes of 'characterization'. In theatre/cinema this is also dependent upon makeup, props, clothes, gesture, body language, *mise en scene*.

3

'You painted a naked woman because you enjoyed looking at her, you put a mirror in her hand and you called the painting VANITY, thus morally condemning the woman whose nakedness you had depicted for your own pleasure. The real function of the mirror was otherwise. It was to make the woman connive in treating herself as, first and foremost, a sight.'
John Berger

The Object

It is still often assumed that a photograph is a reflection of the 'real world' – that we can read off people's faces and bodies simple 'characters' and roles, just by how they look in pictures.

Here, one object, a female doll, has been taken and placed with a variety of different objects in order to demonstrate the changes that take place through different juxtapositionings.

- HOW DO WE KNOW WHO SHE IS?

- WHAT SHE DOES?

- WHAT HER ECONOMIC STATUS IS?

- SUPPOSE WE ONLY SAW ONE OF THESE PICTURES?

The female doll is constant yet the 'image' of her ranges across a whole spectrum of differences.

So what is different? How and why do we read it as different?

Power and Sexuality

'If we say the world of the man is the state, the world of the man is his commitment, his struggle on behalf of the community, we could then perhaps say that the world of the woman is a smaller world. For her world is her husband, her family, her children and her home.

But where would the big world be if no one wanted to look after the small world? How could the big world continue to exist? If there was no one to make the task of caring for the small world the centre of their lives?

No, the big world rests upon this small world! The big world cannot survive if the small world is not secure.'

Adolph Hitler

_U_SING FAMILY PHOTOS IN THERAPY
1983

Much has been written about the ways in which photographs can be analyzed. Very little has so far emerged (beyond the specialist journals of North American psychologists) about the use of our personal photographs in trying to recall the past in a way that moves beyond anecdotal or 'common-sense' reminiscences.

Two of my childhood photos were the basis of an hour-long session of co-counselling, a non-hierarchical, one-to-one, inexpensive type of therapy, with my tutor Peter Clark.

This method of working with photos isn't the same as having a 'rational' discussion or chat with friends or family, nor is it in the mode of anecdotal story-telling about one's past. It relies on a great deal of trust between those involved, few interruptions except to help the flow of thoughts from the past, and a counsellor with no right to analyze, comment, reprimand or offer advice. Although it is more likely that a trained therapist or counsellor can direct your monologue towards such very specific recall of a fantasized past, it might be possible to work with a close friend, sister or comrade. This work is a kind of 'permission giving' session in which you are encouraged to go over old stories in new ways. This should never be seen as pure recall (which is impossible) but rather a way of reconstructing past events so that we can make more sense of them in the light of new knowledge. Although I had done a lot of reading on the history of working class theories of war, and on the way children are socialized into their gender roles and thus positioned in their families in very particular ways, this still did not allow me permission to re-inhabit fearful aspects of how my own sexuality was formed.

So here, instead of trying to 'remember the war' (something we often did in our family), or to pin down the dates of the photographs, we tried to recall why these were two such important and distressing pictures in my life. Why should I have torn them up many times over if my mother had not prevented it? How is it that they are at total variance with my own image of the past as I would ideally have liked to remember it? How are they a constant reminder of all those multitudinous repressions that got cemented over within my family relationships, so that in the end it became impossible to speak to myself about what the photographs really represented? What follows is a transcript from the session.

JO SPENCE: I'm sitting at a dressing table and it's got three mirrors. I love sitting there because I can see both sides of my face and when I tip the mirrors in certain directions I go on forever. There are thousands of me and it's lovely. Then when I put the light on above it I look terrible. Immediately it forces me to realize that it's an illusion because I can see all the detail in the face now and I look tired. That's my memory of that mirror.

PETER CLARK: I'm looking very tired.

J: Yes, like this first photograph. The same kind of 'oh God, I'm not really a little girl face'. But the mirrors are lovely cos you can swing them about. So, I'm looking in the mirror and on the dressing table are glass objects and in them are different things like hairpins and little trinkets. That's just the top of it and it's all very cold and clinical. There's no nice smell, no nice colours, just things. But there is some powder and there is a thing for polishing your nails (but I don't remember her polishing her nails). But when I open the top drawer of the dressing table there is a beautiful jewel case in there, it's inlaid moquette and inside it are all her necklaces and little things that my dad had given her, or that her father gave her. Like a little carved elephant inside another carved elephant, inside another one, all of which are tiny, which he brought back from the first world war, that's lovely and I play with that. And she's got a crystal necklace which I loved putting on. But I've got to be careful with it because my brother has already broken his grandfather's watch (laughs). He doesn't put the jewellery on, he puts on. . .

P: The masculine stuff.

J: Yes. All that stuff would be in my father's wardrobe drawer like a camera, a very old fashioned razor . . . my brother would never try on the things that I'm trying on and I wouldn't dream of playing with the things that my father had. So already. . . And we probably wouldn't be doing that at the same time either. They would be little secret things that we both did.

P: So, I'm sitting. . .

J: So I'm sitting at the dressing table. I know I did it like this. I had to start at the top and work my way down. Then in the two side drawers on each side are underclothes which are woollies and knickers . . . horrible things, absolutely awful things. But tucked underneath are cami-knickers with the buttons that did up underneath. Why would she want knickers that undid underneath? I always wondered about that.

P: Why did she?

J: Why did she? (laughing) I'm not sure I can answer that question. I don't know. I know the reasons why adults like those kind of knickers, they either give you quick access for sex, or you don't have to take your clothes off to piss. But I think to a child who wore ordinary knickers that they were very strange. But they were kind of pushed underneath. In the bottom drawer were woollies and cardigans. Tucked underneath on the left hand side is this thing, which is actually in a shiny red box. It's not just lying there.

P: It's in a shiny box.

J: This is beginning to merge with another image now. My father always had piles and in the bathroom was this other thing. . .

P: This thing.

J: This nasty object that I later found out he used to push suppositories up his bum. There's a nozzle on it, a bit like the nozzle on the thing I'm looking at now. Its *awful*. Jesus.

P and J: Ugh, oh, ow, terrible.

J: What's that got to do with love or anything?

P: Yes, what's that got to do with love?

J: Oh God (sighs deeply).

P: If that's what love's about I don't want anything to do with it.

J: It isn't what love's about. Okay. So. I'm looking in the box. It's a long way from that photograph but it is totally attached to it.

P: Tell me about the box.

J: Yes, I'm trying to avoid talking about the box. There's red rubber tubing that is probably about a foot long, no it's longer than that. It's got a kind of syringe type thing that you can push in. The type of thing we had in the kitchen for lifting oil or grease out of the middle of a roast of meat. You push in the bulb and it lifts the muck out. Oh . . . oh. God it's horrible. Absolutely horrible. At the other end is this nozzle and I don't know what it's for. What on earth is this?

P: Yes, what on earth is this?

J: What's this got to do with the other things in the dressing table? I can't make any sense of it at all. I just think it's horrible. What's that got to do with my mother? It can't be my father's because its in her dressing table. What *do* they do with it?

P: Yes, what do they do with it? (Long, long pause).

J: Oh, I've just remembered what else is in this drawer, sanitary towels. Oh yes, it's definitely the nasties drawer (laughs). I don't know what they are either. And tampax. She's never shown me any of these things or talked to me about them. What are they for? I can't believe it. Everything in the other cupboards and drawers is open to me. But these aren't the same, no one has ever talked about them. Never any other sign of sex in the house but that, now I think about it, coming forward in time. Because once I knew what it was I looked for other signs. What do they do? Why does she want to wash herself out? My father didn't appear to use any kind of contraception. So, what did they do? Of course that was a big joke in the playground, 'johnnies'.

P: Johnnies.

J: Definitely. A lovely word to say, and if you could get hold of one even better. Horrible things. Why anyone would ever want one of those inside them I don't know, I still don't know. Obviously I was a rampant naturalist! (laughs). Moaning about all these accoutrements.

P: (laughing) I'm a rampant naturalist.

J: Absolutely. Why do we have all these things put upon us? There's a kind of double memory now and it's to do with images and feelings. There's the lovely feel of this material; it was all soft when I rubbed it against my face. This isn't out of a Hollywood film. Maybe it is, but I think it's what I remember.

P: You rub it across your face. . .

J: Um. I can actually climb in the wardrobe and smell my mother. I have often climbed in the wardrobe and shut the doors. Not locked them because that would frighten me.

P: Pulled the doors to?

J: Yes, also specially when we were playing hide and seek. It was one of my favourite places to hide. Literally climbing back inside her. God I never thought of that before either.

P: Climbing back inside her.

J: I never climbed inside my father's wardrobe, it was horrible. There were all his dull-covered, no I mean dull-coloured jackets hanging up, and hard shoes in the bottom. Nothing soft in there.

P: Stay with the slip for a minute. 'Everything is dull covered'.

J: Yes. It is. Everything about that bedroom is dull covered. Their bedroom was completely controlled. My father was in the furniture trade. He was a manager in a furniture shop at one point and they had very modern furniture which I always hated. And they had a maple leaf walnut suite in the bedroom, hence the triple-mirrored dressing table, matching wardrobes (hers was twice as big as his interestingly); they both had mirrors in the doors and if I opened both doors at once I could see across from one to the other. And the bed. . . This is quite important, quite important, because I've been photographing bedrooms funnily enough. This bedroom is the most unfriendly room I think I've ever been in actually. The furniture was bought for a much bigger room so it now kind of crowds the whole room out, and they keep changing it around but it never looks right. Whatever you do with it, the minute you open the door it's like being in a furniture showroom. That's exactly what it's like.

P: A furniture showroom.

J: Yes, that's exactly what it's like. God fancy living like that. Living in the suburbs is absolute hell. First of all you are trapped by the houses, then you are trapped by the rooms. Then you are trapped by the people you live with.

P: Trapped.

J: You are absolutely trapped. I have got such awful memories of all this.

P: I was absolutely trapped.

J: I was – absolutely trapped. For as long as I can remember I was trying to get away from it. This is what the fields and going out to play were about. Because that was really about building another life. But people keep interfering with that. It's a good job they do because I need looking after. . .

P: I have a thought of just asking you to say 'I have built another life'.

J: Um, I have built another life. And it's in the image of the things that came later, that I liked. But what I really want is to get back to the nice things about being with them. I don't want to remember just the awful things now. Because I have tended not to remember anything at all. So now I'm going back to what was awful and that's distressing, and it's going to distress my brother I know. But he's got to understand, like I have, that isn't all that happened. And I have a feeling that he and I were great mates a lot of the time. But I also have a feeling I hated him (laughs), because he was my little brother.

P: I hated him.

J: I must have hated him.

P: I must have.

J: Yes. He was a bloody nuisance. He was the other end of it. They were saying 'do this', and he was saying 'do that'. And he wanted to be looked after even more than I did, now I think of it. Yes, that's right. Poor little sod. So he's got . . . God isn't it dreadful . . . two layers of people to get through, he had. Parents that were never there and a sister that was always saying 'look, just go away and leave me alone'. Although I think they were there for him – that's part of my jealousies I think. I don't think I have ever believed that he's been through what I have. There's no way. . .

P: They were there for him.

J: I thought they were there for him.

P: Why?

J: Because I thought they loved him more than me because he was the new baby.

P: They love him more than me.

J: Well I was sent away wasn't I (belligerently)? He didn't get sent away.

P: You got sent away.

J: He did get sent away though the second time. He came with me the second time. Oh God! What must he have thought had happened to him? Because he was only four then.

P: What do you imagine he thought?

J: I should think it was the end of his world, quite frankly. And then when we went to live with another family in Derbyshire – we lived with a mining family – I was so disruptive that they put me with another family and left him with that one. So he lost me then. . .

P: What's the thought?

J: Well, I feel riddled with guilt about it, actually.

P: Talk to him now.

J: What a terrible thing to do to a child – me, I mean.

P: To you?

J: No, I mean for me to do to a child.

P: Talk to him. Tell him 'I'm sorry I did that'.

J: 'I am really sorry I did that to you, but I needed to be a child. I didn't want to be your mum and dad'.

P: I'm not your mum and dad.

J: 'Your mum and dad were left in London, but you're too little. You can't exist without other people. I am already, I've got my own friends now. I have got some smashing friends. We hang around the chip shop together all the time. . .'

This session lead to another during which insights gained from this transcript were mobilized, so that whole areas of family life and my own sexuality began to be articulated. Feelings frozen for years began to surface.

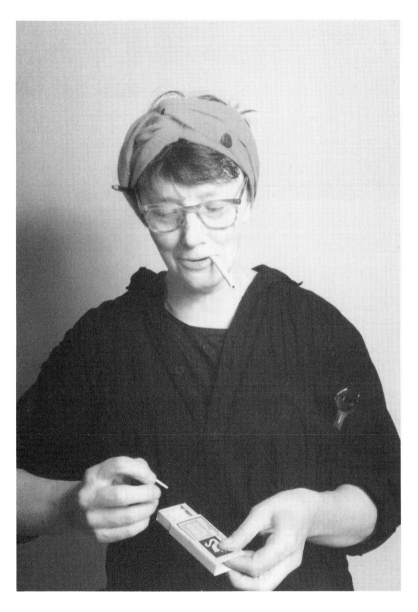

*In a photo therapy session
with Rosy, I go back to a
period in family history
where I felt I had been
abandoned. I try to imagine
my mother, in playful mood,
as a war-worker. What
came to mind in the session
is that at work she could
enjoy the forbidden fag (my
father banned her from
smoking). I am surprised by
the knowledge generated by
this session, especially in
relation to family health.*

THE PICTURE OF HEALTH? 1982 ONWARDS

Four years ago I was diagnosed as having breast cancer. Like so many women before me I submitted myself to the medical machine, going along with the treatment so far as to have a lumpectomy performed. The feelings generated in the circumstances surrounding this were so totally negative that I felt, come what may, that I had to get off the medical orthodoxy's production line. The article 'Confronting Cancer' shows how I felt at the time.

CONFRONTING CANCER

When I was a young woman, living still in the parental home, I became aware that I was Waiting for Something to Happen. Years later, when it had apparently already happened without my even noticing, I regretted the loss of this feeling of expectation. Even later, I realized what it had been – the desire that comes with wanting to fall in love, wanting to be told you are loved, by that special Other. Recently, I realized that the feeling had come back. Not (sadly) in relation to love, but to illness and hatred.

This preamble is by way of approaching a difficult subject. Last Christmas, having recently completed three years' study as a mature student, having earned my first-class degree with honours, now utterly exhausted and wondering what the hell it had all been about, I had to go into hospital. Suddenly.

Dutifully, so as not to waste time, I took with me several books on theories of representation, a thin volume on health and a historical novel. One morning, whilst reading, I was confronted by the awesome reality of a young white-coated doctor, with student retinue, standing by my bedside. As he referred to his notes, without introduction, he bent over me and began to ink a cross onto the area of flesh above my left breast.

As he did so a whole chaotic series of images flashed through my head. Rather like drowning. I heard this doctor, whom I had never met before, this potential daylight mugger, tell me that my left breast would have to be removed. Equally I heard myself answer, 'No'. Incredulously; rebelliously; suddenly; angrily; attackingly; pathetically; alone; in total ignorance. I, who had spent three years (and more) immersed in a study of ideology and

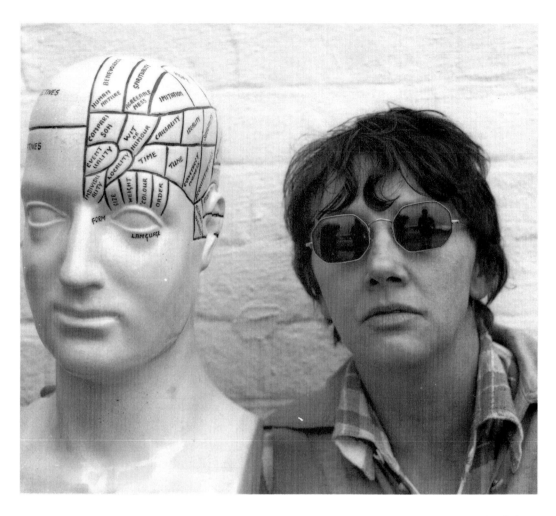

The thinker with no body.

visual representation, now suddenly needed another type of knowledge; what has come to be called 'really useful social knowledge'. Not only the knowledge of how to rebel against this invader, but also of what to do beyond merely reacting negatively. I realized with horror that my body was not made of photographic paper, nor was it an image, or an idea, or a psychic structure . . . it was made of blood, bones and tissue. Some of them now appeared to be cancerous. And I didn't even know where my liver was located.

This peculiar disjuncture in my knowledge of the physical world caused such total crisis in my thinking and activity that it is only now, some six months later, that I am beginning to realize what has happened to me. So began a research project on the politics of cancer, with a fervent desire to understand how I could begin to have a different approach to health in which there would be less consumerism, more medical accountability, more social responsibility, more self responsibility.

Ever since I can remember I have tackled extreme forms of adversity by becoming ill. Usually after the event, I have manifested asthma, hay fever, eczema, colds, flu, bronchitis, depression, lumps and tumours . . . whatever. I am now convinced that these came about because, within the class I belonged to, I had been socialized to neglect myself, materially, environmentally, economically, psychically, even (dare I say it) spiritually. Now I am taking the toll as I approach my fifties of having tried so hard for years to give too much, to perform too much, to be too involved in too much . . . often for the wrong reasons and with the wrong people.

I was aware in my hospital bed, as I took the first step towards defiance of the medical orthodoxy, that it would be a long and lonely confrontation. It took an immense amount of courage initially to say no, that I didn't want to be mutilated (beyond the three vivid slashes that now adorn my breast), or to be radiated or drugged (what in warfare are called 'hack and burn' methods). The recollection that, at 28, I had had an ovarian tumour removed because of the side effects of early steroid treatment for my asthma, and that, now, I could lose first one then another breast, terrified me beyond all reason, beyond anything that had ever happened to me before. The realization that I also had months of waiting whilst I was screened to find out if I was now clear of active cancer equally terrified me.

I took the coward's way out and became a vegan. I tackled my diet first. In five months (following the integrated regime of the Bristol Cancer Help Centre) I have lost four stone in weight merely by eating healthily. I sought out therapists in order to find out how to help make my life more balanced without giving up struggling. I took up co-counselling and learnt how to be assertive rather than aggressive. I regularly visit 'my' psychiatric social worker who has steadily worked through endless problems with me, patiently unravelling my closed off system of logic, my repressed desires. And I found myself a delightfully bolshy socialist feminist naturopath. Now I can begin to hear myself ticking over again. No miracles, no racing motor, no rejuvenated going off into the sunset . . . it's just that I can begin to hear my inner voices speaking to me in ways I didn't realize were possible.

Beyond that, I can still call upon the social knowledge of all the theoretical and political work I have encountered across the latter years of my life. I can again begin to feel solidarity in political struggles, in spite of the total loneliness of defying the medical orthodoxy. No longer am I engulfed with guilt about not working hard enough, not putting on a good enough performance, whether

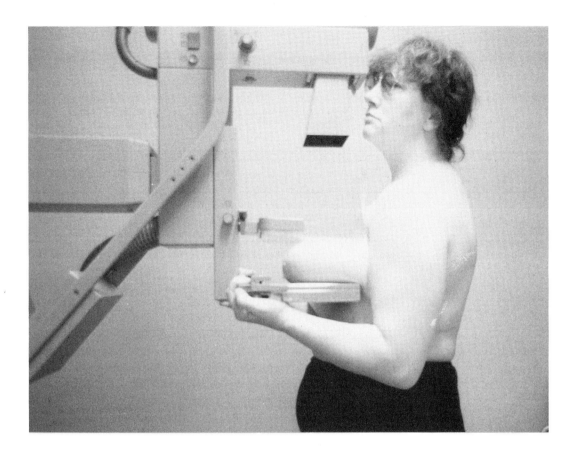

I occupy the correct political position or not, whether this or that latest theory can be lived without. I have had to face the fact that I am totally vulnerable, able to die, to feel terror, to be terrorized ... but able to fight back with the help of others. Thank you, I learned a lot.

First published in CITY LIMITS, 22 July 1983

In the system of medicine for which I finally opted (Traditional Chinese Medicine – TCM), the patient is encouraged to begin to take some responsibility for getting and staying well. At the very least this means more work for the patient, and the necessity to make informed decisions; at its best, it means the shattering of lifelong habits in relation to food, drugs, exercise and breathing, and the awakening of the knowledge that the body cannot deal forever with a completely unharmonious relationship with her psychic, spiritual, social, economic, living and loving conditions. In plain English, I learned to love myself better and get more in touch with my actual needs and feelings so that I could start to try to change things wherever possible. It is my belief that TCM

Passing through the hands of the medical orthodoxy can be terrifying when you have breast cancer. I determined to document for myself what was happening to me. Not to be merely the object of their medical discourse but to be the active subject of my own investigation. Here whilst a mammogram is being done I have persuaded the radiographer to take a picture for me. She was rather unhappy about it, but felt it was preferable to my holding the camera out at arm's length and doing a self portrait.

offers me the best chance of survival as a cancer patient, or at least a better quality of life. It does not pretend to offer me a 'cure', but is a way of managing the illness, putting it at bay, and perhaps slowing it down.

My TCM practitioner is Yana Stajno, whose partner David Lurie prescribes herbs to me on a weekly basis, taking account of my total condition when he prescribes. I see Yana as a traditional female healer, in that she uses her hands, her medical skills and counsels me whilst she attends me. We have a totally professional relationship, yet within it we discuss ways in which I treat her as a surrogate parent while she encourages me not to be too dependent on her. I have experienced love and care from them both which is without parallel in my years of medical treatment by general practitioners and hospital personnel. They charge me on a sliding scale at their lowest fee as such medicine is not available on the NHS. Traditional Chinese Medicine is either picked at as a medical commodity (e.g. acupuncture), or else is sneered at by western cancer specialists, who display an alarming degree of ignorance (and racism) in their belief that their recently evolved treatments are superior to thousands of years of cumulative health care within TCM. In China both traditional and orthodox treatments are available for cancer and patients can (in theory at least) have access to either or both systems.

The regime for rebalancing my whole body and my psychic life is as follows:

- Long term change to a macrobiotic diet with occasional organic white meat or liver, plenty of fruit and vegetables, some nuts and seeds, fresh sprouted seeds and beans and freshly juiced fruit and vegetables

- No sugar, salt, gluten, dairy or animal products, no preserved, tinned or processed food

- Daily Qi Gong exercise, a routine part of cancer treatment in China, to help circulation, breathing and energy distribution, as well as strengthening the body

- Twice weekly acupuncture

- General health care through Chinese medicine

- Occasional lymphatic massage

- Daily megadoses of vitamin C and mineral supplements

- Herbal intake daily (brewed up from raw dried Chinese herbs in my kitchen)

- Monitoring of stress levels

- A loving relationship and reciprocal counselling sessions with David Roberts, my partner in life

- Plenty of cuddles and bodily contact with others

Because I am a photographer, I began to ask myself questions about the way disease and health are represented to us. Given that women are expected to be the object of the male gaze, are expected to beautify themselves in order to become loveable, are still fighting for basic rights over their own bodies, it seemed to me that the breast could be seen as a metaphor for our struggles. The fact that we have to worry about its size and shape as young women, its ability to give food when we become mothers, and its total dispensability when we are past child-bearing age, should be explored through visual representation as well as within health-care. The two should not be separated out in any way, as our concept of sexuality and our social identity stem from both lived experience and the imaginary self we carry in the mind's eye. Just as the female body is fragmented and colonized by advertisers in the search for new markets for products and is fetishized and offered for male consumption through pornography, so it is similarly fought over by competitors for its medical 'care'. There are no departments of 'whole body' medicine in any hospitals I have ever attended. The concept is quite alien at any institutional level, although individual doctors and nurses exist who are interested in such medicine.

Even while I was in hospital, I began trying to represent to myself what was happening to me by using my camera. But how to represent myself *to* myself, through my own visual point of view, and how to find out what I needed and to articulate it and make sure I got it – ultimately wanting to make this visible to others? How to deal with my feelings about myself and give them visual form?

I realized that a major absence in my own family history was any knowledge of what had happened to other members of my family in terms of mental and physical illnesses. Family photo-graphs hide any evidence of illness or ageing, since photographic conventions encourage us to 'smile for the camera' and the lack of clarity in small images prevents us seeing fine detail. I finally made up a health chart of my own life placing banal snapshots against details of diseases and treatments. This led to a decision to visually document my struggle for health and to try to see how that allied itself to campaigns in other fields, in particular, peace campaigns.

I believe it should be everybody's right to take photographs inside all state institutions. So I photographed a lot of what happened around me in hospital. Using my delayed action shutter I was able to include myself in the picture, but I never had the nerve to photograph anything happening to me directly, least of all my appalling treatment at the hands of consultants, which in any case would have warranted a video camera with sound. Terry Dennett and Maggie Murray photographed me at the hands of the NHS and undergoing TCM.

A meeting with Rosy Martin in 1983 led to our involvement in photo therapy, (see next section), which means, quite literally, using photography to heal ourselves.

In sessions with Rosy, I began to work on what I came to call my mind/body split. It had become clear that in documenting my physical progress, I had entirely left aside questions of how I experienced my illness. Through photo therapy, I was able to explore how I felt about my powerlessness as a patient, my relationship to doctors and nurses, my infantilization whilst being managed and 'processed' within a state institution, and my memories of my parents. Later the work moved towards body image, emotional eating and the way parental control worked through diet and feeding patterns. This led on to a visual exploration of the mother and daughter relationship, as a result of which my mother ceased to be the monolith of my imagination and began to exist on many different visual planes, each linked to my memories of her at different periods in her life. The ability to have a dialogue with my imaginary mother (now dead) encouraged me to 'parent' myself better.

In 1985 I enlarged an image/text critique of orthodox medicine which had been exhibited at the Camerawork gallery into a touring show called *The Picture of Health?*. The documentary work by myself, Terry and Maggie and the photo-therapy work by Rosy and myself was contextualized by Jessica Evans' work on ortho-dox medicine, in which she foregrounded the myth of the doctor as hero through images from medical text books, film stills and staged photographs.

Once the exhibition was on the road I felt I could relax – until I decided it might be useful to use it to talk to people within orthodox medical circles. I have now begun a new journey which is taking me to health conferences, women's groups and into direct encounters with medical students. To stand in a lecture theatre in a major London teaching hospital, explaining my experience as a patient and the contradictions between ways in which the medical profession controls women's bodies and the 'imaginary bodies' we inhabit as women, was most exhilarating. Learning new and more subtle strategies, beyond aggression and dogmatism, has delight-ed me and shows me I am moving in a more healthy direction.

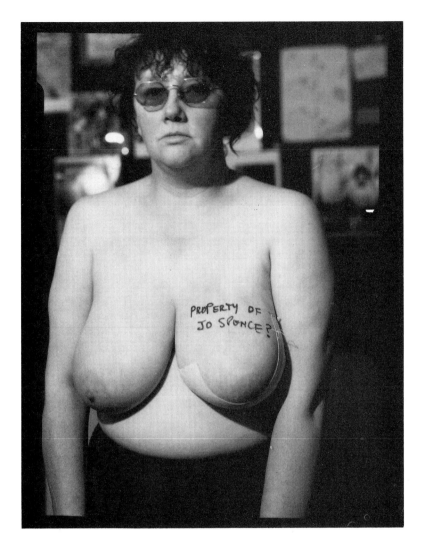

Before I went into hospital in 1982 I decided I wanted a talisman to remind myself that I had some rights over my own body. Terry Dennett and I set up a series of tableaux, each with a different caption written on the breast. This is the one I took with me. I felt I was entering unknown territory and wanted to create my own magic fetish to take with me.

These documentary photographs were mostly taken from the patient's point of view, and this in itself was therapeutic, enabling me to concentrate on what was happening to me in a different way from lying passively in bed. However, such photographs cannot tell us the truth of the diseases from which we suffer, nor where power resides within the medical orthodoxy or how it is maintained. Nor can they tell us why we are so ignorant about our own bodies and healthcare. Giving our bodies over to others to do as they want with them is a form of collusion in our own continuing infantilization.

For other 'truths' about cancer I had to research in libraries, attend conferences and workshops and become part of a network of alternative healing processes. Only then did I begin to understand how power resides in knowledge, and how exclusion results not only in ignorance, but in a belief that there is only 'one truth' about the ways in which the mind and body function. By applying the knowledge I had gained in higher education (most especially from the work of Foucault and Althusser) I began to ask questions about the way in which the institutions and professional bodies of orthodox medicine used photography to help maintain the status quo, and thus retain their power over us as patients.

I asked the women in my ward whether they minded if I took photographs of what was happening in the hospital. I said I wanted them for my family album. No one objected. These are some of the 200 or so pictures I took.

The consultant's ward round. He enters the ward dressed in an expensive suit and is surrounded by a flock of white coated students. When he gets to my bedside I immediately stop taking photographs.

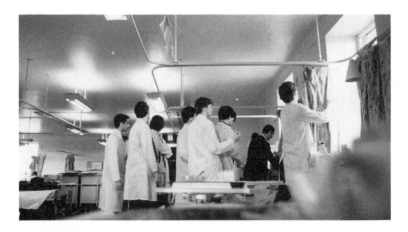

Anxiously waiting.

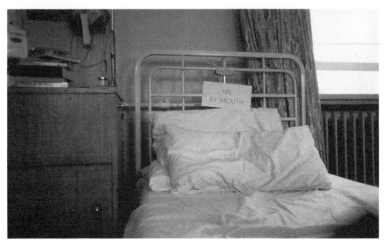

Taken just after my pre-med injection, on the way to the operating theatre.

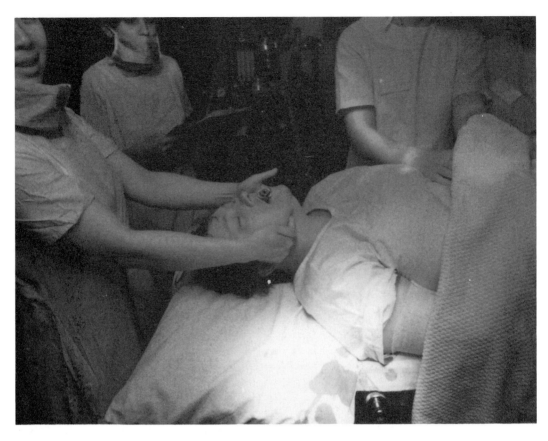

*Taken by a ward doctor who
attended my operation. I am
being wheeled to the recovery
room after the operation.*

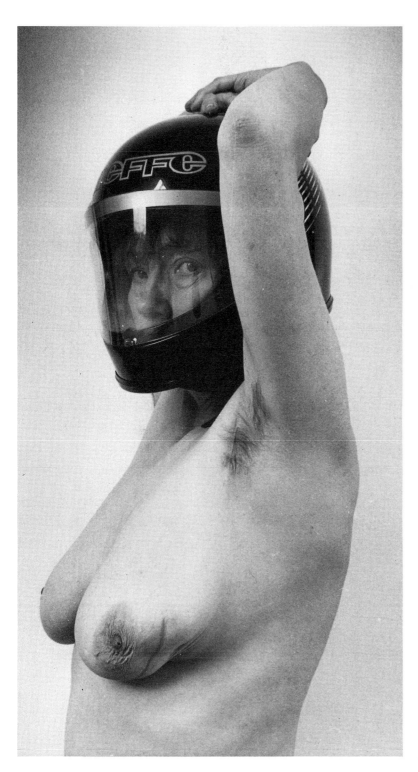

'The analogy between the war on cancer and the war in Vietnam is more than metaphorical. Since the rise of the cellular hypothesis – that cancer is a mysterious, tumorous condition of localized origin – the medical establishment has sanctioned only three methods of treatment: surgery, radiation and chemotherapy. On a larger scale these are precisely the three major weapons (search-and-destroy, bombardment and chemical warfare) utilized militarily against social problems (i.e. political and economic insurrections) in Vietnam and other parts of the Third World.'

ALEX JACK, Cancer Control Journal, vol. 5, No 3/4

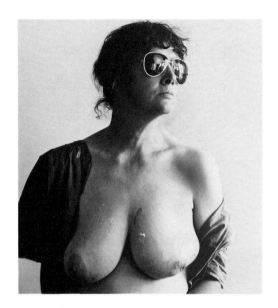

Providing images in order to have a dialogue with myself. The question is 'Will I be a heroine or a victim?'. The answer I gave myself was that I had no desire to be either; I merely wanted to be 'seen' as a person in the daily struggle to restore equilibrium and health to myself.

Patients are usually excluded from access to their medical records, so when I had a liver scan Terry and I decided to take our own image from the monitoring screen. In order to do this we had to get clearance from the hospital, granted on condition that it would not be used for public display.

It felt vulnerable and lonely
being the only person I knew
to have opted for
*Traditional Chinese
Medicine* to treat my cancer.
Although available freely to
women in China, it is
virtually unknown here. I
asked *Maggie Murray* of
the *Format* photographic
agency to document my
healthcare. Maggie agreed
to provide me with such
prints as I needed for my
own and exhibition use, so
long as the negatives could
be lodged at Format and
made available to people
interested in a view of
alternative health care. I
found this a very
satisfactory arrangement
and feel, as a feminist, that
women involved in
something they feel worthy
of documentation should
approach groups like
Format and offer
suggestions for new subject
matter to be made visible.

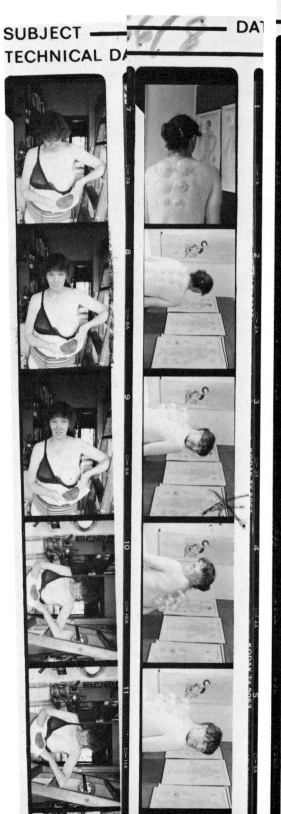

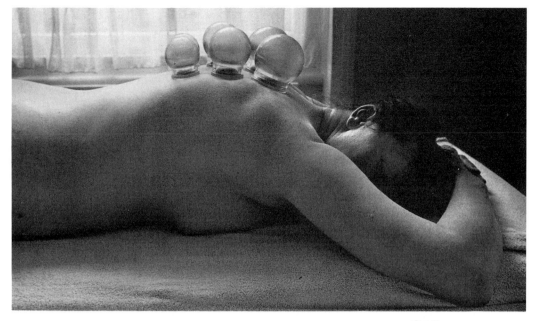

Cupping.

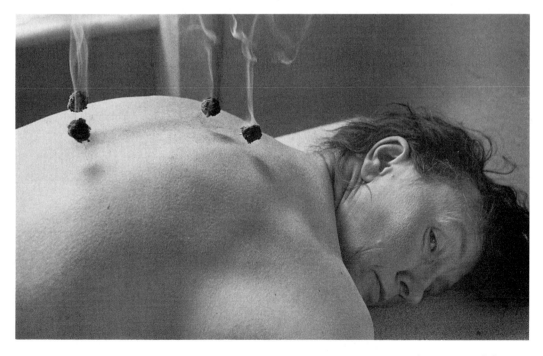

Acupuncture with the burning of the herb moxa on the top of the needle.

Women attending hospital with breast cancer often have to subject themselves to the scrutiny of the medical photographer as well as the consultant, medical students and visiting doctors. Once I had opted out of orthodox medicine I decided to keep a record of the changing outward condition of my body. This stopped me disavowing that I have cancer, and helped me to come to terms with something I initially found shocking and abhorrent.

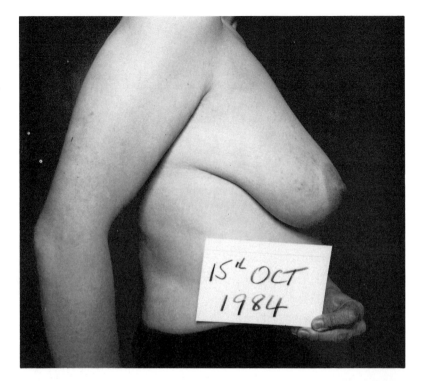

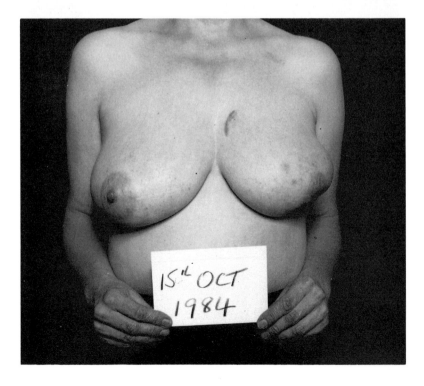

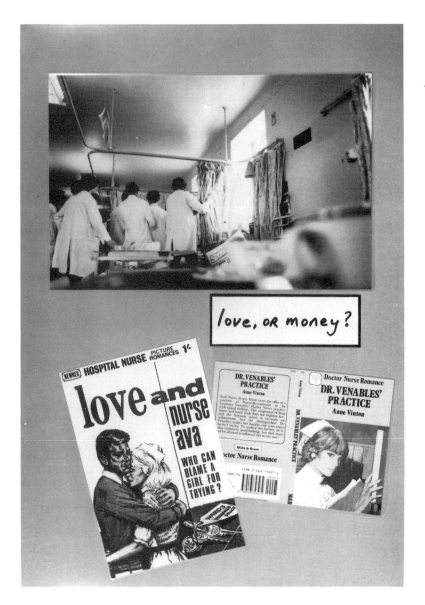

Adding a documentary photograph taken by Maggie Murray into images of my fragmented body which had been written on and staged for the camera in a photo therapy session with Rosy Martin. My aim is to try and form a bridge between work done on health struggles, usually dealt with through documentary photography, and work done on body as image. An understanding of how these spheres relate seems to me essential to being healthy and well-balanced.

The Picture of Health?
is a laminated touring show which is now available for use in health and media groups. There are two versions – one for galleries, and one for more informal venues. This work was grant-aided by the Greater London Arts Association.

*Working on my mind/body
split in a photo therapy
session with Rosy Martin.
But more of this later.*

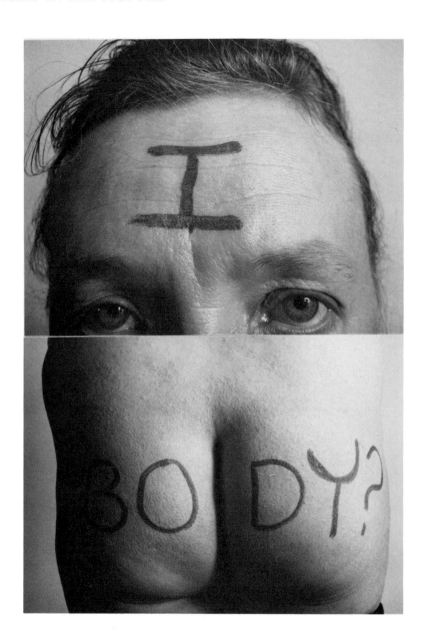

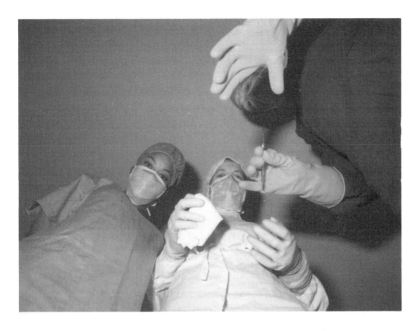

Doctor and nurse romances are well established as a literary genre. Here I am looking at the scenario from the patient position. From this prone state of powerlessness it no longer seems inevitable that the nurse 'will gaze at his aquiline profile whilst he held the tiny trembling heart in his surgeon's hands', nor that the doctor will eventually succumb to the wiles of the nurse. They become instead the all powerful figures of the child. in the nursery, and the crossover between mummies and daddies and later authority figures becomes more apparent.

From Remodelling Medical History, *a project in progress by Terry Dennett and myself. We ask the question, 'Whose reality is this?'*

PHOTO THERAPY: NEW PORTRAITS FOR OLD
1984 ONWARDS

Rosy Martin and Jo Spence

We have been developing our own form of photo therapy in the last few years. Traditionally, the portrait is typified by the notion that people can be represented by showing aspects of their 'character'. We understand the portrait differently. Instead of fixity, to us it represents a range of possibilities which can be brought into play at will, examined, questioned, accepted, transformed, discarded. Drawing on techniques learned from co-counselling, psycho-drama and the reframing technique borrowed from neuro-linguistic programming therapy, we began to work together to give ourselves and each other permission to display 'new' visual selves to the camera. In the course of this work, we have amply demonstrated to ourselves that there is no single self but many fragmented selves, each vying for conscious expression, many never acknowledged.

We believe that we all have sets of personalized archetypal images in memory, images which are surrounded by vast chains of connotations and buried memories. In photo therapy we can dredge them up, reconstruct them, even reinvent them, so that they can work in our interests, rather than remaining the mythologies of others who have told us about that 'self' which appears to be visible in various photographs. The point where image production in society intersects, through our snapshots, with personal memory is where a disruption can be caused, so that we never see ourselves in quite the same light again.

The reframing technique we use is a kind of internal permission-giving. Permission to change, to re-view, to let go, to move on. It is not a way of discussing the 'real' to see if it is 'biased', but of finding new ways of perceiving the past so that we can change our attitudes and activities. Through the medium of visual reframing we can begin to understand that images we hold of ourselves are often the embodiment of particular traumas, fears, losses, hopes and desires. Once on the psychic 'operating table', we can begin to work on these areas. We are talking initially about changing the images in our heads and hearts, but we both passionately believe that a first step for us as individuals

towards broader social and economic change can be this facing up to the limiting defence mechanisms and blocks which we inhabit and which pattern us. We are all locked into past histories of ourselves of which we are largely unaware, but by using reframing as a technique anything can potentially be turned on its axis, words and images can take on new and different meanings and relationships and old ideas can be transformed.

In the sessions from which these photographs were drawn, we worked to produce a series of different, constantly changing, images of ourselves. We started each time with an idea of what we wanted to disrupt, replace or rework, and then worked loosely within this framework.

Integral to this work is a shared politics of feminism and demystification of photographic practice. As feminists we take it for granted that current dominant images of women should continually be questioned and if necessary challenged, but we find the notion of 'positive' images a limited one in that it ignores how

Rosy and I begin a photo therapy session in which we examine the silences and absences of our school photos.

meaning is constructed or subjectivity produced. We prefer to explore the more dynamic construction of images in order to understand the cross-over between what feels personal to us as individuals, and what is public and given currency and wide circulation. For women, the question of looking and taking pictures is determined by the dominant culture. Those who create, circulate and own the image production processes, thereby define and control their meanings. Along with others, we are attempting to re-invent and then reclaim the pleasure of looking and of image production and circulation. We hope that women of other races, ages, sexuality and class will engage with the process here. It is based on mutual aid.

Rosy Martin writes: photo therapy is about transformations and change. It challenges the fixity of the photographic image and the search for an ideal self. By creating a wide range of images I have been able to examine many different aspects of myself and my past history, and to integrate these into a whole. By acknowledging aspects of myself and my past, which I might otherwise hide, or see as my 'shadow' side, I have freed myself from internalized restrictions and oppressions, and have come to accept myself as I am, complete with all the contradictions that have formed me. Photo therapy is photographing feelings, in all their rawness. It is a means of shifting the understanding of concepts from the cerebral intellect to the gut. I have found that certain issues and ideas which I thought I had worked through and understood, for example in relation to my mother, could still produce feelings of angst. By making images of these feeling working with Jo, I have been able to integrate my intellectual knowledge at a deeper, unconscious level, to transform it into an inner wisdom.

In working on myself as a child, my starting point was a photograph from the family album, which I carefully restaged. I wanted to show the child that lay behind that 'good little girl' image, which is the only one that appears in my family album. I wanted to examine, recreate and transform this construction, to reclaim myself as a child, in all her aspects, to take back the power I/she had, the capacity to be creative, autonomous, joyous, independent – as well as angry, grief stricken and vulnerable.

In recreating myself as my mother, my starting point was a studio photograph. In the process of taming my hair, and painting on the tight narrow smile of the martyr, I remembered the messages she had repeatedly given me, 'I gave up my life for you. Never get married'. I touched the emotions of limitation, restriction and unfulfilled ambition, which I know to be hers. I was no longer dealing with feminist theories of mother/daughter relationships, but living through the feelings evoked by the responsibility of putting other people's needs first, never getting what she/I wanted, and teaching her daughter the contradiction both to be like and to respect her, but not to choose the same life as her.

I have examined the social construction of myself as a young heterosexual woman, to show what an un-natural, extra-ordinary distortion was required of me in order to take up the expected position. By recreating a tiny fragment of memory, a small detail from everyday life, ironing my hair in order to straighten it, the act of denying who I was in order to be acceptable to others is made clear. Through the politics of feminism and my shift from heterosexuality to lesbianism I have become aware how my adolescent self was socially constructed. Through photo therapy I can acknowledge that I colluded in that, and can make visible the strange rituals and masquerades which I adopted. I can thus challenge the concepts of a 'natural' heterosexuality.

Other areas of my life that I have most productively worked on in photo therapy with Jo include becoming my father; the schoolgirl; class and education; health and smoking; the gendering of images; lesbian stereotypes; power and powerlessness; and retelling myths.

Photo therapy is a way of examining one's social and psychic construction, both emotionally and theoretically. By supporting each other, and working cooperatively together, sharing, taking risks, accepting, allowing depths of feeling in front of the camera, we have been able to use photographs to ask questions. Photo therapy is entirely about processes, rather than fixed products. Although my work is rooted in my personal history, arising from my particular experiences, it contains resonances; our traumas and pains as women are not identical, but are identifiable. In sharing our work with others, Jo and I have found this recognition.

This work exists within a framework of debates on media studies, history, feminism, therapy and memory. The work takes up and questions many of the themes of photography itself, challenging the concept of the 'decisive' or 'perfect' moment, and the 'truth' of the photographed image. It exposes the image production process, working against the grain of existing mythologies, for example of family photographs, looking at everyday events and small details, challenging 'fixity' and rigid social roles. The work decodes sexuality and gendering and begins to show them as social constructs.

In these pictures Rosy Martin is the subject of her own material, whilst I act as photographer/therapist. What is shown here is only the tip of an enormous iceberg. We have produced two exhibitions on photo therapy and are preparing a book.

Who constructed this child?
Mum, Dad, Hollywood?
The photographer?
Transformations
The child in me.
Me as child.
The child I contact for my work
The child others find unacceptable
The child no-one else should see.
The child that no-one chose to photograph.

Rosy Martin

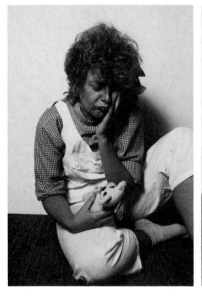

My Mother

My first love.
Here I wanted to see her
Autonomous
before (she mothered) me
yet already a mother,
To look at her-story
To exchange with her.

A studio photo
posed smile,
Yet she appears at ease
within herself,
Stylish, elegant,
neat, smart,
Perfected, precise,
Tailored by her husband,
Presenting proudly
her two sons,
Wife mother
(both this woman and those
roles)
unknown to me.

To become her
I tamed and smoothed my
hair,
narrowed and painted my
lips,
Proud and placed,
Yet I felt uneasy,
tense, (s)mothered
constrained, restricted,
prescribed by a role
of elegant responsibility,
weighed down,
burdened,

'I gave up my life for you,'
'Life is hard'.
'You will not get what you
want',
'Be happy'.

I emerge
untamed
and shake myself free

Rosy Martin

In the construction of heterosexuality it's the little details of life that count! By re-creating a fragment of memory, a whole new set of meanings can be opened up.

Dashing away the smoothing iron

*Doing the ironing
imitating my mother,
Later transforming
my curly locks
to straight,
to become loveable,
to find someone,
to love me,
for whom
I can do the ironing!*

Rosy Martin

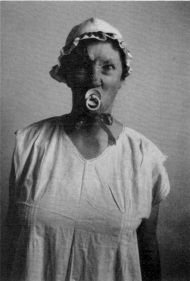

The following pictures are of myself, taken by Rosy Martin acting as photographer/therapist.

Restaging the drama of going into hospital and being infantilized.

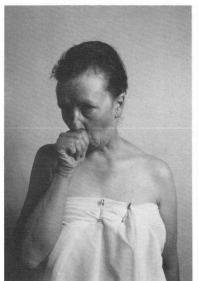
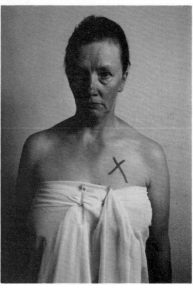

Making an icon of 'live food' (part of my new diet) in a photo therapy session with Rosy.

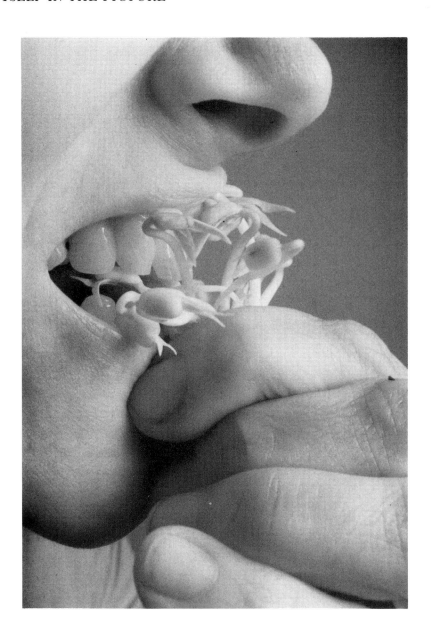

Transformations

As a child
I did everything
possible,
not to be
like my mother.
Family Romance?
Cinderella,
Ugly Sister, Fairy –
I tried them all.
On the other hand
(now using my brains)
I still try to please
surrogate daddies.
Again, I fall.

Ageing, angry,
alone, ill,
I regard
the constellation
of imaginary selves.
Finally, with joy,
I picture
my dead parents.
In memory
I can be them,
Moving beyond
the past
I become

My own parent.

*Working on the emotional
roots of patterns of eating,
with myself as both subject
and director of photography.*

The wedding photographer who watched herself being watched while she failed to understand her own history.

This chart we have compiled compares the dominant practices which surround the portrait and our evolving practice.

PORTRAITURE

- Photographer has control
- Traditional methods of encoding used

- Replicates a known ideal
- Naturalizes
- Closed, flattering
- Product based
- Universalizes
- Image 'improved' and manipulated
- Single image, chosen from many
- Single stories
- Makes statements
- Freezes in time

- The 'perfect moment'
- De-historicises

- Concentrates on special events
- Makes sweeping statements

- Stereotypes
- Confers 'status' and 'importance' (respectability); offers image of social mobility

- Reinforces stereotypes (blocks our perception of ourselves and others)

- Constructs definitions of 'ugliness' whilst creating, defining and fetishizing beauty
- Self hatred

PHOTO THERAPY

- Sitter and photographer create together
- Evolving methods, working against the grain

- Transforms
- Exposes the construction of the 'natural'
- Open ended, revealing
- Process based
- Particularizes, personalizes
- Image production process exposed
- Multiple images, narrative fragments
- Matrix of narratives
- Asks questions
- Opens time out; looks at past, present and future

- The perfect moment is challenged
- Places you back in your own history, and allows you to ask questions of the dominant discourse of history

- Looks at everyday events
- Shows important tiny details, and thereby validates them

- Shows individuality
- Examines power and powerlessness

- Unblocks perceptions; gives permission to change

- Allows us to examine our failure to live out such fictions

- Self love (making portraits for ourselves)

- Assumes heterosexuality

- Repetition of dominant cultural fantasies

- Encourages the search for an ideal self

- Offers us phoney wholeness and harmony

- Encourages rejection of multiple selves

- Offers only surface appearances

- Reinforces symbols, eg power, beauty, stars, heroines

- Offers possibility of the 'desired' image. Narcissism is unquestioned

- Ideas conventionalised

- Colludes to help us present a public face

- Self denial (portraits are invariably made for other people)

- Promotes ignorance

- Hides/blocks

- Closes down on feelings

- Reinforces anxiety about 'looking right'

- One-way communication

- We collude to fool ourselves

- Shows little regard for feelings and thoughts of the sitter

- Suspicion

- Expensive

- Opens up question of how you explore or express your sexuality

- Allows exploration of 'good' or 'bad' self in fantasy

- Encourages the acceptance of a spectrum

- Allows an examination of the fragmentation process

- Positively encourages the acceptance of a split self

- Attempts to seek out and identify structures

- Old symbols are explored, enjoyed, reworked and subverted towards finding and creating new symbols

- Reveals the possibility of exploring the desire and pain inscribed in such impossible images

- Ideas bounced off each other become more lateral

- We collaborate to make visible and share private inner selves

- Self acceptance

- Encourages self knowledge

- Reveals/unblocks

- Opens up and encourages acceptance of feelings

- Reclaims women's pleasure in looking through recognition and release of anxiety

- Two-way dialogue

- We cooperate to help ourselves

- Works with the feelings of the sitter, to give those feelings a visible form

- Trust

- Cheap

Excerpts from a discussion with Valerie Walkerdine about photo therapy.

VALERIE WALKERDINE: Do you feel that deconstruction as practised in the academic arena has become sterile?

JO SPENCE: When as a mature student I entered the realms of theory, I knew I could deconstruct 'the family' until the cows came home. But of course you cannot just deconstruct something and put nothing in its place. The irony of deconstruction was that although I felt in one way in total control, in another way I lost control completely. I took my belief system to pieces until I began to fall to pieces myself because there was a divorce going on in my family and I was in the process of deconstructing my sexuality theoretically, and for all that one would wish to understand that one is a divided subject, frankly I was no longer able to get up in the morning I was in such a major identity crisis. Basically you cannot deconstruct without a reconstruction process going on simultaneously as it does in photo therapy, where each time you deconstruct you are already at the beginning of the next phase of putting things together again.

VW: A continual process of transformation?

JS: If you have a problem you need strategies for solving it. Deconstructing may clear the myths away, but you still need strategies. I can't just proceed in a negative way. I can deconstruct orthodox medical practices, I can deconstruct the image of the doctor, but it doesn't tell me how to improve or redefine my physical health. For me that element is missing in the deconstruction model of the world. I want to be part of that area of education which encourages people to think for themselves, to understand not only the process of how the unconcious mind works, but to find out where to go for information and how to know if it is in your own or your group interests. Unless there is some notion that change is possible, then the act of destroying illusion is in itself insufficient.

In relation to my own health project, I deconstructed the dominant image of cancer, and in taking it to pieces I realized what I needed to find out about other discourses. But if I had merely deconstructed the disease as a theoretical concern, and done nothing else, then I could be dead by now. You are on the road once you start deconstructing, there is no doubt about that at all. But if it is only an academic exercise, with no links back into the actual needs of individuals and groups at specific times, then where are we going?

VW: Can I pursue the relationship of your illness to deconstruc-

One of a series of pictures I took of Valerie Walkerdine during a photo therapy session.

tion and how this seems to you to be part of a journey toward healing?

JS: Rock Hudson left a fortune of $22 million – yet he had been unable to purchase a cure for AIDS. The fact that somebody with all that cash couldn't solve their problems is a terrifying prospect for a sick person. Take that as a text. This means that the 'natural' fact of AIDS is that whatever you do you will die. Well that is a completely fatalistic statement, and as we know from other reports reaching us from America, some men have now begun to take affairs into their own hands with vitamin and mineral therapy, and stringent health food dieting and exercising, and are getting rid of their illness. There are parallels in the reporting of cancer. Because I had learned to research and take things to pieces, I looked for a discourse of cancer in the newspapers: I wanted to see how the medical profession sold its truths. I kept cuttings on it, and very quickly could discern that what passes for 'news' is in fact a series of public relations exercises to keep certain ideas in the public domain which both offer apparent hope for the future and thereby help reinforce the power of the medical and pharmaceutical industries, but at the same time they also help to whip up more and more hysteria about the disease. There is a continual barrage of 'new' information, but if you approach a hospital and ask for the 'miracles', of course they don't yet exist. If I had not learned how to take things to pieces, then I would not have gone to look for another 'truth' on a quest for knowledge for survival.

I'm not saying that because you have other knowledge you can rid yourself of the disease. I am saying that armed with new knowledge you are able to make choices to act rather than be acted upon. But only if you have 'unblocked' your beliefs, your perception of what is 'true'. To try to change 'habits' as ingrained as how you inhabit your body or your construct of the diseases you suffer from, appears a monumental task. However, within socialist philosophy we are taught to go back to the tiniest detail, the smallest everyday habit like sprinkling salt on all our food, and learn something new about it. Unless those small habits are examined and taken seriously there is no way that anybody can consider taking on much larger problems, like cancer. The problem is that we live in a culture that tries to do things by magic from the consumer's point of view. We are not involved at all, things are either done to us, or for us. Our education and health is provided by the state, therefore we don't have to worry about it, our labour is categorized and taken from us (manual or intellectual), we are offered identities to inhabit by the media. In taking on board ways of changing our own perception of health and of gaining more control, we are facing power in its most pernicious form. If you believe the dominant idea that doctors cure us of illness but that even they don't know what to do, then you have a completely fatalistic set of ideas in circulation. That is a political question.

VW: How does the photo therapy help you towards a more positive mental attitude?

JS: Ever since I can remember I have been angry with my mother but suppressed it, and latterly when she was older, suppressed it so much that I actually didn't like her at all and had even forgotten the anger. The last thing I ever wanted to be was like

her. When my mother died of breast cancer that absolutely confirmed it for me!

Early Mother

But part of what has happened in my health project was a retracing of those steps back to when she died, to accept that I was implicated in her death. I helped to kill her. I was one of three people who put her out of her misery. I felt no remorse or sorrow or anything. All I felt was total relief, not for her, for me. After the event I went back and rationalized that the relief was for her, but at the time I now remember that it was for myself. Photo therapy made it safe for me to go back to childhood. It is easy to act out being a child and be cute, but to actually go back and experience what you felt is incredibly frightening. When it did happen I began to think, 'Yes, but what was it like from *my mother's* point of view?', which is something I had never done before. She never had a point of view in my fantasies. So in the next photo therapy session I decided to be her. And because it was me at five or six years old, the point at which I can place my first conscious anger, it was around a scenario of abandonment. 'You don't love me. You sent me away. Everybody else is happy at home except me. I'm going to make myself ill in order to get your attention, so you'll have to take me back.' Going back to being that child and then reversing the point of view, I now realize that she must have felt terrible herself, something I had never been able to accept before. To be the mother who lost me is incredible because it has opened up a whole side of me that was blocked off. When I was six I was evacuated for the second time, leaving my mother and father at home with a young child. At the time she was quite ill with pneumonia, and the reason I got sent away was because she couldn't cope with all those things as well as an active six year old who was going to school in the blitz. But of course I understood none of that at the time. Even when I researched representations of women in World War II and found that mothers were encouraged to send their children away by the state, I never got anywhere near my anger towards her. As a piece of research, it could never deal with the fantasies and pain around being sent away.

So now I had moved on. I had taken up my mother's point of view and could accept that she was desolate when I was sent away, as well as relieved. But that didn't alter the fact that as a much older woman she still totally disapproved of me and my lifestyle. I lived in a respectable, working-class, upwardly mobile family that never made it. I was their hope in a sense. They were delighted when I became a photographer. My father even paid my first quarter's rent so I could have my own studio. But my 'disapproving mother' goes back to a particular episode when I was twenty when I went to a party, met a guy and went to bed with him, and was so scared the following morning that I decided to run away from home. But I didn't run away, I just didn't go home, and I spent the whole weekend with this group of artists, just hanging around and having a nice time. Something unheard of in our family. On the Sunday evening my boss found me in a coffee bar and dragged me out, dressed me down like he was my father, and took me back to my parents. All the way home I worried about what I was going to tell her because I knew that she would know 'what I had done'. Of course she never addressed it directly, just had general hysterics. That for me was the conscious beginning of never wanting to talk about my sexuality. So I learned to live a double life, and as she got older and older (in my fantasy) her mouth got more and more tight and went down at the corners. So I only had to see her face to know she disapproved. So finally in photo therapy I felt brave enough to become that mother, too. I made her really sneer at me, turning the mouth down so much that it became ridiculous and I burst out laughing and stuck my tongue out.

When I got the photographs back I realized that I was looking at the way in which I sneer at myself, my internalized parent who says 'Don't do that, that's not very nice' for a whole range of things.

Late mother

I next became my mother in the war, the mother I left behind when I was sent away, a war worker with a life of her own. My class history comes out here because immediately I started I knew from memory that my parents had to get up at 5 a.m. to make their sandwiches and flasks of tea. So the first shots I did were of my mother making the sandwiches which I had never thought of in forty five years. Then I passed on to being her at work in a boiler suit and turban – straight into stereotyping because I never saw her at work. I began to feel that for her work was a release from home into the comradeship of women. I set up some shots of myself rolling up a cigarette in a fag machine and having her first fag of the day. And as soon as I did that, I realized one of the reasons why she had bronchitis so often. I had never made the connection. I then set up my dirty hands, getting the grease off with Swarfega, and finally I am her in a pinny and jumper, neatly at home getting the tea. I have allowed her to be a young woman. I have destereotyped her. The fun side of her is coming out. The later mother has now softened in memory as a result of showing her to have had a life of her own that pre-dated my projection of her disapproval.

VW: Do these shifts in your perception of your mother come about when you take up the pose?

JS: Not exclusively. There is an ongoing self-reflexive process that continues as more and more pictures are produced, (which incidentally parallels the experience of putting the *Review* together and perceiving links and obsessions I never saw before). The moment when I get to be her for the camera always needs a lot of preparation. There is the initial stage when I give myself permission to do what I want. Then the gathering of props, usually done by going round the charity shops as I have nothing left of hers at all. The first time I felt awful, like I was tainting her memory by pretending to be her by wearing other people's clothes. Then I had to get over the mother in my head saying she wouldn't be seen dead in that! My mother was always present, but never in a very constructive way. But when I take up the pose I start to remember my relationship with her. I did not realize I had a memory of her making sandwiches for the factory. It seems so trivial that it is hardly worth thinking about. Yet it is a key thing in a Brechtian sense, a gesture that is coded into our class position. I can't imagine middle-class children watching their mothers making their sandwiches before going off to the factory.

The day I get the prints back I lay them out many, many times, usually on the floor. And of course they are as much to do with me as they are with her, and at last I am able to examine my feelings for my mother. All sorts of feelings are coming up and being dealt with and allowed through, because it feels safe at last. The pictures are a vehicle in that sense. If it is unsafe I can say to myself 'well, it's only me anyway' – That is the beauty of photo therapy.

VW: What are still the taboo areas for you?

JS: I think for me they are around looking at women's bodies. I could never look at women stripping off in my studio. The first time I saw a man's penis in my studio was a completely different thing because of my own relationships with men. Dolls are pleasurable to work with for this reason because you can displace and disavow as much as you like. Dolls are a useful way to explore pornography and the idea of the woman as the object of the male gaze, as we found in the Polysnappers group. They saved us from ethical problems of ripping off the model or of providing voyeuristic images. All the same, they have their problems. I remember setting the naked doll up in a room with a window built in to imply that somebody was watching her. She was in a spotlight, somebody was (in fantasy) in the room behind the cut-out window, looking at us, and I was looking through my camera at that. So

there were three looks in operation. Whilst I was doing it somebody walked across the studio, and I felt like I had been caught
with my hand in my knickers. I don't think if I had been working
with a male doll the same thing would have happened. It would be
totally different.

*'Preparing to be a beautiful
lady' at the age of 52.*

VW: How far is the relationship between doing the looking,
holding the camera, and the problem of being looked at, the
problem of your own sexuality?

JS: Well for me, in consciousness, the problem of being looked at
has always been around masturbation, that was the absolutely
forbidden subject as a child. And so therefore that is something
which I hid and would continue to hide. I think my conclusion
around that was that my genitals were something to be ashamed
of, and I think that catching sight of other women's genitals is a
double-edged thing – there is the possibility that I do desire them
and I want to suppress that, but also I want to see how they
compare to mine. Because if they were not the same as mine then I
would be the 'inferior' one, because there must be a hierarchy as
there is with other parts of the body!

But that's another story. . .

*T**HE FEMALE GAZE*
1985

Being 'taken ill' in 1982 was possibly the most eye-opening
experience of my life. It took me on a journey in which I sought out
and experienced many different kinds of therapy. Some of these
therapies I used intermittently, some only once, some I commit-
ted myself to in my struggle for health. They included learning to
co-counsel in pairs and groups; solo therapy with a psychiatric
social worker; working with a Jungian cancer therapist on my
mind/body split; attending workshops on Reichian bodywork;
attending Neuro Linguistic Programming sessions (NPL) in relation to health and belief systems and then doing part work and
using reframing techniques with an NPL therapist; working with
feminist notions of deconstructing the social and the archetypal
and looking for 'positive' ways forward; attending health conferences dealing with the psychic and the somatic in illness. I came to
realize that each one could be seen as having different (though
sometimes overlapping) ways of conceptualizing the psychic and
the social through visualization techniques, visual fantasies, and
image making. It was a short step to realizing that photography
could be used in relation to many such therapies.

As students we were offered a vast number of theoretical texts
on psychoanalysis, relating mostly to film theory, which we were
expected to integrate into our practices as still photographers.
This I found impossible to do, and could only apply theory to
existing imagery in an endless round of deconstructions of texts
'out there'. Now after my years of photo therapy with Rosy, I feel I
can add something to the theories linking psychoanalysis and
photography.

The idea of the patriarchal gaze, of the male 'look' with the
woman as its object, has been well theorized. What has been less
theorized is the idea of the female gaze. Putting it bluntly, the idea
that women are not expected to look back, are expected to be the
exhibitionists, still dominates much theoretical thinking. Whilst
working as photographer/therapist with two men, I have recently
begun to experience what could be meant by the idea of the female
gaze. In the safety of a photo therapy session based on mutual
trust, with no value judgements, no interruptions and no inter-
pretations, it began to seem possible that whilst I, a woman, was
in the therapist position, my 'sitters' could begin to give visual

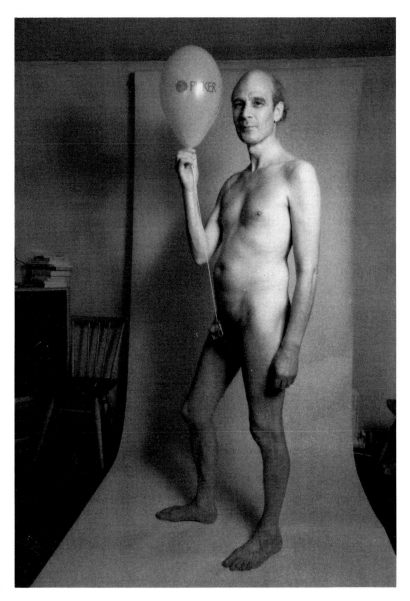

expression to their feelings about aspects of their sexuality. Either to live out what they had repressed or to try to broaden their definition of sexuality.

Each man had a totally different visual approach to his sexuality. One, working within a Jungian framework, presented himself in symbolic fashion (what in psychotherapeutic terms is termed the 'transpersonal'). In giving expression to deeply felt longings and anxieties about the fixity of his own masculine construction, he felt it would be productive to try to work through how it felt to become female (the bringing together of the male and female selves within the one greater self). This was done by making huge symbolic drawings of an archetypal mother, then entering the womb and becoming the foetus, finally emerging to be born 'female'. A series of images was produced which followed a transformation through symbolic childhood into puberty. Another session dealt with a regression backwards through a symbolic evolution of humankind into a 'freer' animal state.

The other sitter worked more from within a Freudian framework. We re-entered the realm of his family history, and through the playing out of all the familial positions (mother, father, child) within a specific scenario, we were able to establish that he could easily take up all these different positions one after the other in visual and verbal form.

Within the safety of having explored himself in the 'victim' position of the child in relation to the mother, we could then begin to take more risks. Here the female gaze seems of paramount importance. In his re-enactment of male childhood I could not avoid being positioned as surrogate mother. But my being in that instance a non-punishing, non-evaluative mother, made it safe for him to enter the realms of sexual fantasy and sexual difference. Thus we were able to see visual evidence, through body positioning and gesture, of the bisexual child blocked off within the adult.

I have been able to help give rebirth to aspects of these sitters' childhood sexuality. Both of them were able to display their bodies to the maternal gaze/camera in a sexually ambivalent way. Such ambivalence held out the promise that they could grow to take the position of the father, and could eventually move beyond the realms of merely pleasing or possessing mummy, or that a choice was possible which would not automatically preclude an intimate relation with a man. I maintain that none of this would have been possible to explore with a male photographer, who would represent a double threat of punishment to the sitter, for desiring, pleasing and showing off to the mother and for the transgressive revelation of homosexual desire (or perhaps even the desire to be female). In both instances this work was part of a transitional phase to other understandings of more generalized potential within themselves.

The female gaze is always foregrounded in working with Rosy. In working back through my adolescence with her, a major area of family 'silence' became apparent. It was only when working to make visible patterns of eating as a form of control, that it felt safe to begin to make the connections between my mother's martyred complaints about my 'never being home on time for meals', and the ways in which she implicitly tried to control and silence certain expressions of my active sexuality. (A complex rela-

Detail of Father (*after David Hockney*).

tionship between her perception of herself, projected on to me, and the grind between my perception of what seemed potentially possible within the culture at large, and what was allowable within my particular family.) With Rosy positioned as the seeing eye of the surrogate mother, I felt fear rising inside me as I presented myself to the camera coded as 'sexually active' teenager (often this could be something as simple as undoing buttons, or giving a knowing look to camera). Possibly the fact that Rosy is a lesbian made this journey safe; working with someone who has fully explored their own sexual choices offered a safety not always apparent between heterosexual people. The fact that I had work-ed on my own homophobia also helped.

Working through and accepting the pain of the construction of our individual heterosexuality was an astonishing process. Un-picking tiny details which had before seemed irrelevant brought into focus major patterning in our lives. Instead of talking in generalized terms of masculinity and femininity, we came to see and feel how our adolescent years had been a very specific construction of a very specific aspect of heterosexuality.

For Rosy, this meant trying to cross as quickly as possible from being positioned as child into an adult, and for me it meant trying to hang on to so-called childhood. Perhaps because I was afraid to lose my playful, less responsible side and take the plunge into openly active sexuality? Once I had worked through some of my material with Rosy on adolescence (and for both of us this took on board the reconstructions of ourselves in terms of class as well as gender), and felt the safety of her non-critical acceptance of what I presented to camera, it became easy to move backwards into re-enacting my so-called oral, anal and genital phases for the camera. This is something which I would find unthinkable with a male photographer/therapist. A benign female gaze was what we both needed to re-experience. Our joint process of re-inventing and remapping aspects of childhood forms the core of our exhibi-tion *Double Exposure – The Minefield of Memory*.

I feel I am no longer an onlooker or critic of patriarchal theory, but have become a participant within developing aspects of feminism in relation to the theory and practice of psychotherapy. In order to understand we first of all have to feel safe enough to deconstruct. We then have to put the pieces together again and again, continually montaging until we make new connections which will enable us to break out of the psychic bonds which hold us. Out of the broken pieces of the self will come a subjectivity that acknowledges the fragmentation process, but which encompasses and embraces the parts and brings them into dialogue with each other. Out of this, for me, has come new activity, new acceptance, and changes I never considered possible.

I have begun to reassess my private life and have learned to reinvent myself within a new relationship. Although I was stimulated and educated beyond belief by the years I spent living and working with Terry, I feel in retrospect that I totally neglected both his and my own needs in our missionary zeal. I forgot how to be loving and I forgot to meet my own needs.

Therapy has enabled me to open up the frozen waste of my relationship with my mother and father. In meeting David Roberts in 1984 and, later, sharing my life with him, I learned for the first time to talk openly to a man about my fears, fantasies and longings about sexuality and family life. Coming from a family which always locked bathroom doors, had silent bedrooms and forbade explicit talk of sexuality or bodies (beyond endless discussions of family illness), I always felt this to be a totally taboo subject. Perhaps, in part, this explains my desire to 'look'. Maybe I just never knew that as a girl I wasn't supposed to do so!

Now I enjoy playing out being the child to David's parent, or mother to his child, or facing up to a whole range of 'parts' of ourselves which have never been released

from their tombs before. We have no children of our own, but have been able to get in touch with a galaxy of childlike selves which we are slowly translating into photographs.

David allows himself to be used to represent the 'patriarchal body', though sometimes he says that I am just using

him as my little Barbie doll. This body changes every time we photograph it. Representations of power can be negotiated at every level of society if only we know the strategies to use. We don't have to wait for the revolution. Changing the image of the family should be a

first stage priority for all those interested in demystifying power. Not because we want to lay yet more blame on our parents (for they are as caught in webs as we are), but in order to try to understand the levels of censorship which exist, and the self-restrictions in operation.

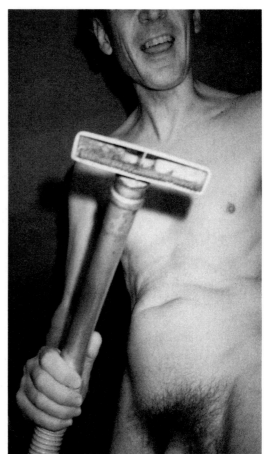

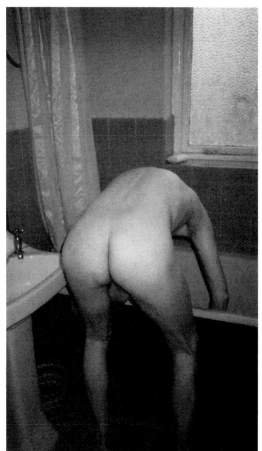

Creating and using photographs within my relationship with my partner David, we re-enact together screen memories from our separate childhoods.

I glimpse my Dad through the bedroom door. (David)

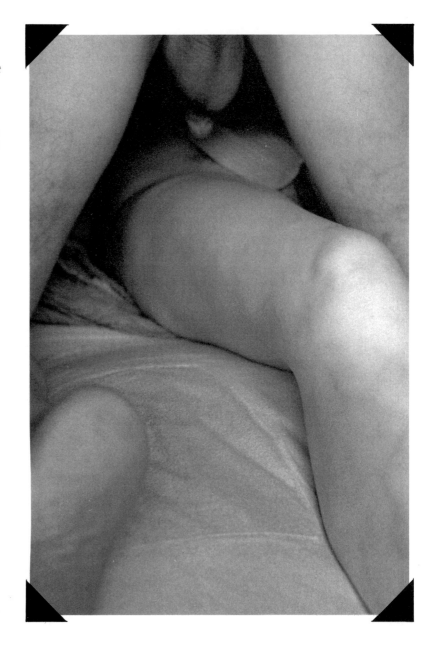

My Daddy washes me (Jo)

*S*OME QUESTIONS AND ANSWERS
1985

In conversation with audiences in various parts of the country whilst *The Review of Work* was touring, the following questions came up.

Do you see yourself as an artist?

When I was a mature student at the Polytechnic of Central London on an arts degree course, we had a lot of lectures about the history of art, as a result of which I decided I was a photographer and not an artist. If sometimes it helps me to get a small grant by calling myself an artist, then of course I will. I finally called myself an educational photographer, whatever people think that means, as a way out of the problem. Then there is the other word 'feminist' that gets tacked on, i.e. feminism as a style of photography, and one could spend the next hundred years trying to explain that it isn't a style but to do with a body of ideas. Although I am a feminist and a socialist I am not a feminist or socialist photographer because I don't think you can talk about photography in those terms.

In 1975 when some of the galleries were getting interested in so-called 'radical work' or interventions made by women who were politicking around certain issues, some of the work like the Hackney Flashers Collective and my own work on personal photographs was elevated onto the walls of the Hayward Gallery. Then it started to be attacked for what it was never supposed to be in the first place. All the bourgeois critics really got their rocks off. So I have a lot of problems around the word artist. All the same, I can't deny a deep inner need now to be acknowledged and taken seriously.

So why did you decide to show your Review *in art galleries?*

I wanted women's work and collective work to be seen in a gallery situation. Lurking behind that was also the fact that I was quite ill and felt it would be nice to see all my work on display together in my lifetime. It sounds a bit desperate but it isn't. My work is usually all scattered about. Some of it has gone into mixed shows. Some of the Polysnappers work has been seen at the ICA in London when they did a show on advertising, and some of Terry Dennett's and my work went into various touring shows. But it has never been seen in its own right, it's often taken off the shelf like a cultural commodity to fill a gap. The Cockpit Gallery circulates many of the exhibitions I've been involved with around schools, community centres and conferences – all campaigning circuits and educational sites. Reviewers persistently ignore group work, especially from the women's movement and from students. Unless it is circulated round galleries, group work is not taken seriously. I'd also like to join the ranks of those trying to redefine the gallery space; some of this work might shock people who visit galleries because it is involved with things like divorce, cancer, sexuality and domestic life.

Do you see a difference between gallery and educational circuits?

Not in terms of money. With very few exceptions, neither artists nor cultural workers make money. For most people, putting on an exhibition is like running a business in deficit. With the grass roots political circuit (youth clubs, further education colleges, campaigns, conferences) you are lucky if they pay for transport let alone damage (panels often get lost, come back with corners torn off or covered in coffee and beer stains). With something like the Hayward Gallery you get £150 to produce your section of the show from scratch. At one end you are a cultural worker and not expected to need fees or budgets and at the other you are an artist, badly paid and reviled by critics. Where cultural workers get their wages from is a mystery to me. Similarly with artists, but at least there is a kudos in some circles for being called an artist. Most people teach I suppose. Somebody like me wanders, without a category. In a sense I don't want a category. I like being moving target, I feel I'll survive longer. But it does mean that the work becomes invisible because people don't know what to do with it, how to label or review it, and, very often, how to use it. It's either bad art or very complicated education! Either way, the circuits for work are very small. If you get something shown on television, twelve million might see it, but if we counted up the number of people who see our work in exhibition form I feel we would give up.

You don't present your work framed as 'art'.

The whole idea of blowing something up and putting a frame round it is an anathema to me, and the idea of transporting frames from one place to another is nonsense in political terms. A photographer colleague said you should be able to put an exhibition in the post if you really want to circulate it. Everything I believe in that respect comes from the early days of making exhibitions where I often had to put a show on a train, Red Star, for hanging at a meeting the next morning, so you had to have things laminated. When my work goes to a mixed show it is sometimes hung, ready laminated, inside a frame, because it would look peculiar alongside other work. Lots of photographers now have this problem of cross-venues. It has made me realize that if a lot of work which is blown up and shown in galleries was made small and put ten to a panel, you wouldn't give it a glance. Often by working small you denigrate your own work, but of course my aim is to show that anybody can do it. The only work I have ever framed is the sequence I did with Ed Barber of a man slowly turning into a woman in front of the camera. The panel I put it on fell to bits, so I enlarged each picture and mounted and framed it. I couldn't believe it was the same work, it looked so exciting blown up.

It has been said that your work is about transforming practice and working collectively. Yet the Review *seems to contradict that.*

Usually photographers are talked about in terms of their development, but most photographers I know have a range of practices that coexist at one time. At college I worked in a group in order to have solidarity as we felt so isolated as women. But I also worked through the same period with Terry Dennett in Photography Workshop and I also went on working on my own.

Authorship is a complicated concept. Some of the work I put together is not strictly my own as lots of other people contributed to it, like Terry, who has done a lot of photography at my request which has now become invisible. Anyone I have worked with could take the part of the work they have contributed to and put it with 'their' work. On the other hand, I can't deny that I come from being a solitary photographer. Even when Photography Workshop was set up I went on being 'me' within it. I believe you have to take account of the fact that you are influenced by the dominant and antagonistic culture you move in, or by the theoretical work you are involved in. The fact that I was born working class and lived through World War II moving from family to family, school to school, determines my underlying attitudes to everything, including photography. It is important for the viewer to know that my work is race and class specific and that I am a woman of a certain age.

I'd also like to point out that collective work poses special problems. It is the quickest way I know to become invisible and not appear within histories of your own subject. No one really knows who all the women were in the Hackney Flashers Collective as it never got written down until now, and we didn't sign the work we sent out on the road as students. No record remains that such work took place or that groups are continually forming and splitting, which is my experience.

What was the major discovery you made from putting the Review *together and looking back over your work?*

You can see the slippage, the movements, and you have to accept that your work is a process and that you can't continually try to find the perfect practice. It doesn't exist. A snapshot might be the perfect practice in a given situation. I was struggling for the perfect practice. I sought to be a 'good daughter' all over again, to perform and please people with this so-called perfect practice. It is not that I was told to do that, but that my internalized parent figures continually sought for me to follow the old patterns.

At times when I was assembling the *Review* I wanted to destroy the earlier work, almost to destroy the evidence – just as we do with our own family photographs. We try to arrest time by snatching ideal moments out of it in the keeping of images of ourselves as women, and we try to destroy what time has done to us, try to hide the fact that we are ageing, wearing out, ill. We are taught as children to hide everything of which we are 'naturally' ashamed. A constant theme in my work has been that of coming to terms with the fact that shame is a social construct, that there is nothing natural about it at all. What in class terms I was taught to be ashamed of (my lack of wealth, my lack of knowledge, my lack of finesse), I have needed to get beyond, to work through, in order to see my own strengths. When I became a studio photographer in Hampstead I was ashamed of my origins, so I tried to pretend they did not exist. I didn't put on any kind of front, but I literally became a 'high class' photographer and worked for middle class people. Working class people hardly ever came to my studio because of its location, the type of pictures I took, and presumably my charges.

How difficult was it to photograph a divorce?

Every taboo is operating while a divorce is in progress. Just as there are taboos round domestic life (witness the paucity of the family album) so when the family splits up the agenda increases, especially when children are deliberately kept in ignorance. I took several hundred pictures of my brother's divorce and then had a crisis about how I could use them. I couldn't use them for anything he didn't want me to talk about and I couldn't say things that the children didn't know. It acted as a metaphor for the way in which events are represented in the media, where certain aspects of power struggles are absent through censorship, or just unrepresentable in pictures. I was careful to include things like the labour exchange, the house being gutted, the children moving out. . . . it is not just a record of the battlefield of human emotions.

You use your own very personal photos to explore certain general things that happen to women. Why do you use yourself in that public way?

Although I was born into the working class, I gradually moved to occupy a different position away from my parents, geographically, emotionally and ideologically. Mostly through the men I knew who were, without exception, middle class. Through the music I liked, the reproductions of paintings and the kind of furnishing I bought, the films and plays I saw, I made the traditional journey of being socially mobile through culture. When I got involved in the women's movement, a group of us photographed some women in factories. Although we achieved our object, I felt very uncomfortable about celebrating this. I think this was because the women workers were very much like my mother and I felt accountable to them. I became so self-critical that I decided I couldn't go on doing that kind of work, certainly I couldn't sell it for a living. I couldn't put my own words with it, couldn't speak for those other women, however much they collaborated, and I almost gave up photography. It seemed to me there was nowhere else to go. But then I began to read stuff published by Centerprise, people's autobiographies. Whole areas of debate on people's history were opening up, and to me it seemed that I could come back into photography through my own family photographs. I could investigate them to try and see what they told me. In the process of looking I came to the conclusion that they told me very little – which is what *Beyond the Family Album* is all about. They were either decisive movements in my life or else, through their genres and styles, part of an aesthetic history of photography. The more I worked on them, the more I concluded that if that was my history, it was a complete mythology. Theory entered here and showed the way forward. Without realizing it I had become involved in questions like 'Can you photograph the real?'; 'Is there a real?'; 'What are you doing with a camera?' In *Remodelling Photo History*, Terry and I explored the theory of woman as object of the male gaze, using myself as the model. I have always hoped that some of my ideas of using the camera might be interesting to others; I have always wanted to encourage others to use the camera for its unfixing, rather than its fixing abilities.

Another reason is that I grew up in consciousness-raising groups in the women's movement where experience was shared.

Your cancer photography, like so much of your superficially bleak subject matter, is actually very positive. Is this intentional?

The work is about the process of struggle when ill and acts as a metaphor for all struggle. I think we should try to represent the struggle for *becoming* well and not just throw up a new breed of victims and heroines. The work should be about the fact that most adult women, for most of the time, are in the control of doctors for one reason or another, and many never experience good health once they start to have children. Our photographic work should show women trying to have more control over their bodies, as part of women's struggles generally to have more control. I want to pass on what I have learned to my nieces, so that if they are unfortunate enough to be chronically ill they will not see it as 'only natural' but be able to ask questions and perhaps change the course of their lives with new knowledge. I hope to throw up all sorts of new types of knowledge, about, for instance, how to confront doctors, which is something almost impossible for most of us because ideologically speaking they are seen as authority figures and surrogate daddies.

How much of your self-exposure and autobiographical approach is to encourage women to explore their identities and histories through photography? Is this part of your politics of photography?

I'm claiming that the camera can be reappropriated. Most people have a camera in the family, yet the way most women are encouraged to use it in the dominant photographic press is utterly banal. At most they are encouraged to photograph their children – but only in an idealized way. When you talk to women's groups about amateur photography, you find it is difficult for them to give themselves permission to even listen to the fact that they don't have to limit themselves to naturalistic photography of the family, that they can actually stage things for the camera or attempt a dialogue with themselves or take different sorts of photographs. It is even difficult for women to engage with the fact that what is normally invisible could be taken up, and that the domestic use of the camera could open out this sphere of invisibility. As soon as that gets through there is general excitement – something like photographing 'a day in the life of' instead of merely the high spots. Part of the work I did as a high street photographer was to make *invisible* the work that women do. I did that all the time without knowing that was what I was doing. I was too busy producing madonna and child images. Now if a friend asks me to photograph her with her child, I make a point of photographing the clutter, the so-called trivia of childcare. It is not so much naturalistic clutter I look for as symbolic clutter, where certain things are brought together deliberately for the image. The next question is how to use such a picture – the redefinition of *use* for amateur photographers. The idea that you might want to talk with your daughter when she is fourteen about your life together when she was small is very far from most people's consciousness. You can suggest that people take photographs of different subject matter like funerals or illness, but in the end you need a context for the use of such pictures.

Photography can also be used to encourage women to take a more political view of their family history. Nina Kellgren and I have devised a set of questions around areas of what you actually know and remember as opposed to what you can allow yourself to speak about. For instance, lots of people in a family know about domestic or sexual violence but no one talks about it. Our strategy was to get women to tell us what they knew and what they normally wouldn't talk about *before* we asked them to talk about their family photos of holidays, weddings and special occasions. We wanted to show them that they actually knew a phenomenal amount about themselves and their families which they had never written down or told anybody. We feel that women already keep the family archives and that it would not be a big step towards keeping them more thoroughly or differently, with a wider political and social context.

How can the representation of woman and minority groups in the media be changed?

I still meet women who don't have the faintest idea about the debates that have gone on or the work that has emerged in photography, cinema and video in the last fifteen years. If you talk to a feminist sociologist there is no guarantee that she will have any knowledge about the debates on theories of visual representation. A picture to her is just something to illustrate a text. There is a time lag between different disciplines.

People who make moving images have unions and organizations which have women's sections or have taken up women's issues. But photographers, by and large, have nothing like that. The most that can happen is that they can belong to the National Union of Journalists, if that is appropriate to their work, where they can lobby around issues of representation, though they are marginalized in the sense that there are so few politicized women members.

I think one has to be very specific about where it is possible to intervene and organize and where it isn't. As a mature student on a photography course who could I have worked with? Do I help set up a women's group, do I tackle the curriculum by tackling the course tutors, do I do a piece of work about education, do I do a piece of work about photography, do I intervene in the exam situation by tearing up papers? Is there any point in joining the National Union of Students when it is not interested in the politics of representation, something which interests me passionately?

It's very difficult to form solidarity when there is no women's cultural centre, nowhere to organize around. You try to educate critics and those in galleries but you run out of energy. I see myself as an old person by the standards of any people going through college now. Who am I? Some fifty-two old woman ranting on about her so-called private life. Sometimes I think the work has to come first. Fifteen years ago when women photographers came together, there was nowhere to hang the work, no funding, it was not recognized as having any validity, and so we worked together for solidarity and tried to give the work a public face. But there was no institution into which we could intervene ourselves; the work itself went off and did the intervening. It still does.

How can you change things when there is no way of making a living doing your kind of photography?

When Terry Dennett and I were researching into the hidden histories of photography, he discovered a very interesting model which was not in the standard histories of photography, called Worker Photography. It had its peak in the 1930s among the anti-fascists in Nazi Germany. People at work and in neighbourhoods organized themselves in groups to photograph their own lives and to service the labour, anti-fascist and women's presses with their photographs. They learned how to teach photography to other workers, if there was a strike they would have a strategy for taking photos of police intervention, if there was a political clash they evolved strategies of how to get the film away without it being seized. Mostly they worked in the documentary mode, occasionally they used photo montage or set things up for the camera. Anything that was terribly complicated was out because of the urgency of what they were doing. I found it a very interesting model of photography because it does not presuppose that you earn your living from photography, but that you earn it in some other way, and use photography as a tool in struggle. It hasn't been taken up particularly in this country for reasons I don't understand, but it seems to me a useful role for women to bear in mind within areas of struggle in unions or institutions.

   Though there doesn't seem to be a problem about portrait photography as a job for women, what is missing is the notion of a high street photographer who is politicized, who has her portrait skill as part of her range of practices. A lot of money is spent on sick people, sick in inverted commas, who are labelled as neurotic or incapable. There is no reason why women should not set themselves up as photo therapists to work on women's self images or their inability to 'speak' about certain things. My own practice is an attempt to answer the question. I am trying to show through my work that there are many alternative ways of using photography to the high street conventions which most people ape.

T HE WALKING WOUNDED?
1986

During the years in which I was involved in a range of cultural interventions and activities, I became a completely fanatical workaholic, dedicated only to the struggle to help make the world a 'better place'. In the process I just about burnt myself out, finally becoming totally confused about who I was actually doing *anything* for and breaking down, both mentally and physically. When, eventually, I ground to a total halt, I shut myself away for a month and cried incessantly. That same month I was admitted to hospital.

I yearned to be a 'good' academic (another working class fantasy), yet my 'constituency' remained firmly rooted in the more informal politics of the women's movement. I found it difficult to move quickly into the world of theory with its dense, short-cut language, and its time-consuming programme of intense study. I wanted to be a 'good feminist', yet I still felt I had to find ways of pleasing the 'marxist' and 'post structuralist' men in my life. I found very little encouragement or solidarity as a woman within the world of academia (which is a rat race like any other) and felt completely isolated and marginalized. Additionally, like other students, I was still trying to address the demands of my own internalized parental figures. In short, an utterly impossible crisis of identity occured. As a result, my ability to continue as a photographer dwindled away. I am only now beginning to find my own voice, both with image-making and in my writing.

During my student period, whilst I was crossing the bridge from the empiricist to the theorist side, I felt as if I had been trampled on (I still do). Various projects I worked on were either too complex (comments from the reactionaries) or inadequate (comments from the avant-garde). Or, even worse, work was ignored. The ultimate brush off. This eternal to-ing and fro-ing between audiences was finally, I believe, a major factor in a crisis of how to use language. The end result was my silence.

How to survive, plough one's furrow in an individual and yet social way, appease everybody, continue to be critical, pay the rent? Quite clearly it is impossible. So I gave up 'professional' photography and become an 'amateur'. For here, I honestly believe, is the (largely ignored) sphere which could have the most far reaching and profound effects on current debates on photography which seem to have reached a stalemate.

JO SPENCE PHOTOGRAPHER AVAILABLE FOR DIVORCES, FUNERALS, ILLNESS, SOCIAL INJUSTICE, SCENES OF DOMESTIC VIOLENCE, EXPLORATIONS OF SEXUALITY AND ANY JOYFUL EVENTS

If the glorious technicolour world of Kodakology could begin to be challenged so that people could understand that the very roots of their being are stitched into certain forms of documentary naturalism stemming from that most treasured of all family possessions, the family album, we could then all begin to breathe more easily. But how can this happen when, from the moment we can hold a book and nod in the direction of small rectangles of coloured paper, we continue to be encouraged to believe that all the complexities of the submerged world of family life can be encapsulated in snapshots, that such pictures 'mean' what we are told they mean, that we are who we are told we are? No wonder it takes an intellectual explosion to shift that perception. Or a major disaster in our lives which causes such a disjuncture in our belief system that we begin to ask new questions.

Much theoretical work on photography has relied on psychoanalysis and theories of sexual difference as a basis. It has been suggested that the workings of the mind lead us to have only certain conscious perceptions about the everyday world, and that the unconscious mind (out of our apparent reach) moves across a matrix of structures and fantasies. How does the blocking off of earlier traumas and desires from childhood, which we still inhabit as adults, encourage us to collude in the limited amount of stories in circulation about family life? Just how much is the lack of image-making about the family part of this cementing-over pro-cess? How does the family album relate to the regime of images offered to us from birth, in learning to read, watching television, acquiring the habits of taking for granted the 'truth' of the stories on offer in the media in general? This regime not only encourages silence from us as individuals around the power struggles between parents, and between adults and children, but positively invites us to enjoy the extraordinarily few stories in circulation about that world.

Whose version of family life do you inhabit in your family? How do you know anything about your own history – most of all the history of your subjectivity, and the part that images have played in its construction?

How comfortable it is to accept the few threadbare old cliches on offer at every level of signification when we are encouraged to be consumers and not critical producers of imagery from the word go, involved as we are in a 'product based' culture, and not one in which processes are explored in their own right. How can we then move from the so-called 'private world' of the family, with its paucity of self imagery but plethora of 'mass produced' imagery, into the world of state, industrial and economic power? How can we begin to make new connections?

Photography can only attempt certain things compared with other media, but its radicality lies in the fact that we can produce, possess and circulate snapshots by ourselves, for ourselves and amongst ourselves. It is there in the high-technology-but-low-cost of amateurism that the future of photography lies for me. If we truly want to democratize how meanings are produced in images, we need to realize that all those practices available to the profes-sional, from the high street portrait photographer, through to advertising photography, to avant-garde image/text art photo-graphy can all be appropriated right into the living room. If we could learn new ways of using our cameras we could start by telling our own stories in different ways. Initially we could use the camera for a dialogue with ourselves, as in photo therapy, to de-censorize ourselves, or as a type of visual diary-writing. Once we feel it is safe to proceed we can share our 'new' stories with allies, and we can begin to re-imag(in)e who we are, both visually and verbally. If we were encouraged to do this as children, who knows what we might begin to make of the world by the time we became adults? One thing is certain: the meagre and partial view of social and psychic life presently on offer through image making and photography would quickly become clearer.

At £1.15 for a roll of 24 exposures of colour negative film (at Sainsburys), with processing at £2.05 including a set of prints (at Bonusprint), we can begin to explore and explode the structures of shame, guilt, loss and desire into which we are currently stitched, and which position and bind us as class and race members and through the construction of our heterosexual identities. Obviously, though I have offered here some examples from my own work, this is essentially a private activity and should be seen as such.

Since I was a student I have begun to rethink how best to use my photographic and political energy. It is no longer practical to jump on a train to Bath (or wherever), rattle off a lecture to a largely hostile audience of tutors and unwilling students, hold a seminar with the few who bothered to surface from the compulsory sessions, leap back onto the train, get to bed at midnight, wake the next morning early, rush through a cup of turgid coffee, sort out a set of slides, pick up my camera, rush across London, negotiate a piece of work, do the shopping, half-write an article on the bus going back, eat a sandwich whilst running between one discussion group on photographic theory and another on the politics of childcare, go home exhausted, eat a cold meal, fall into bed next to the man I love, but have seen very little of, etc. etc.

In retrospect I can only say that I am not sorry I did the work I did (and will go on doing in a more considered and leisurely way) but just wish I had paid more attention to the warning signs that my body and mind were giving out. It is sad that even though I had made a study of semiology, when my body 'spoke' to me with her various 'signs and symptoms' I could not understand what was being 'said'. I write all this because I now see more clearly how others are treading the path I did. Never stopping to take stock, over-committed and undernourished, vitamin deficient, totally stressed, always in some conflict-situation or other, exhausted, propped up on chemicals and junk food, cigarettes and alcohol. Treating colleagues, students and family like shit – but, politically, okay! Even though cultural and political struggle will continue (and is more important now than ever) it is also essential to take account of our own personal needs.

As a newly-minted middle-class woman who is involved with cultural and ideological rather than economic struggles (though it must be said I would starve to death if I tried to live off what I earn from such work), I feel it is still most useful that my time and energy be deployed to problematize power relations in the places where I find myself. Hence my current work around health and in the domestic sphere. I believe I can best intervene in the everyday places with which I am familiar, not look outside to 'help' others. People are always telling me that I am brave to 'expose' myself in the way I do. I don't agree. When you act in the light of knowledge which is in your own self-interest or in the interests of your group or class, this is not bravery but absolute necessity.

Long live amateur photography! Long live the healing arts!

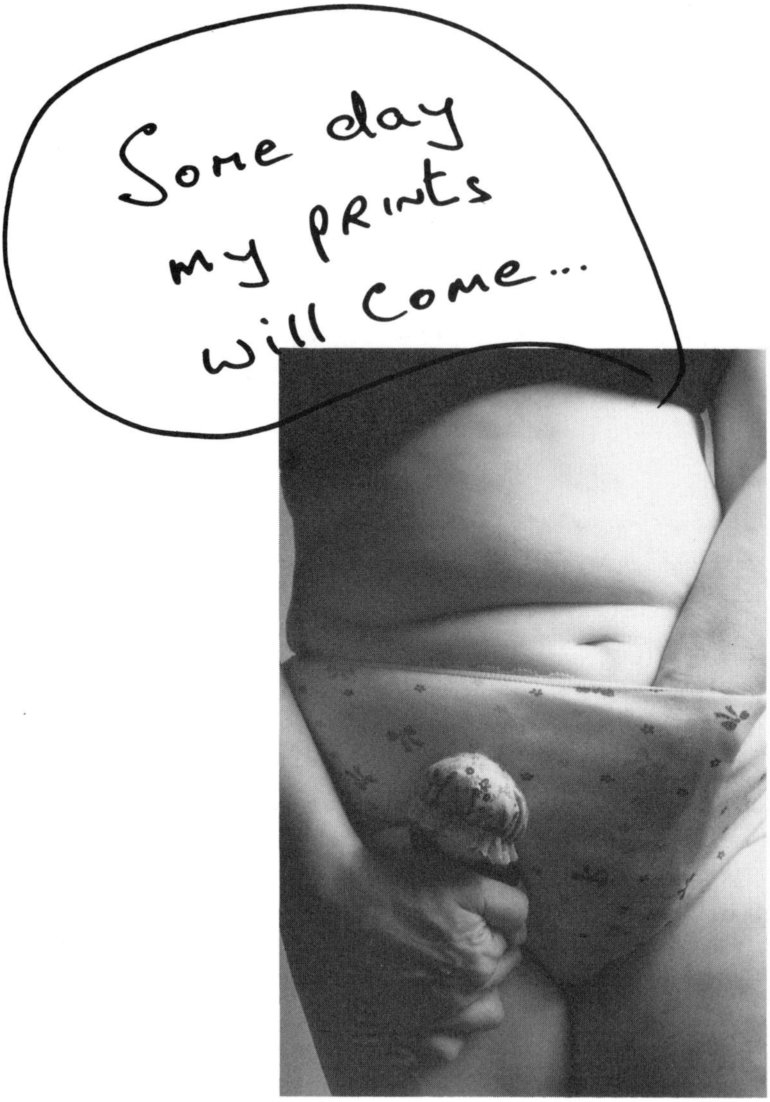
Some day my prints will come...

Jo Spence,
Wembley, Middlesex

Sept. 18, 1985

Dear Frankie,

Thanks for your letter. I never know whether to call you Frankie or Frances, so I'll put one version on the envelope and another on the letter. But let me tell you a story. . .

I was born Joan Patricia Clode. Quite happily that stuck (except for being called Cloudy and Clodie at school) until I went to work where there resided another Joan. So immediately I was christened Jo. It stuck. Of course other people who met me after that had their own variants – Josie, Josephine, Joanne, Joanna, Jojo, YoYo, Josikin etc. etc. Then at 30 I married and became Joan Patricia Holland. But called Jo Holland (except by the DHSS). Then I left my husband and went to live in Ireland with a man named Neil Spence. I went to a commissioner of oaths and took the name Spence. But I forgot to change the Joan to Jo. God knows why. So now I was Jo Spence. When I came back from Ireland we split up (having declared eternal love for each other some twelve months previously). I then went to live with one David Phillips. By now alerted to the vagaries of my sexual and love life I decided to stay with Jo Spence. Except that I started a business and decided that Jo Spence sounded a bit naive. So I called myself Joanna Spence Associates. That way, I felt, I could charge proper professional fees. Some years later, David and I broke up, but not before I had made a will in his favour.

Some years even later I went to live with Terry Dennett, and stayed for eleven years. Last year when I was ill I decided to do two things: 1, to make a will and 2, to get divorced. Just a matter of tidying things up you might think. At that stage I was married to Keith Holland, and left all my worldly goods to David Phillips (whom I didn't know had already died), and lived with Terry Dennett. All I wanted was a quiet life! After I had got my divorce and made my will I fell in love with one David Roberts and moved here to Wembley to live with him. I can't be bothered to change anything else (and recently found out that my husband had died anyway) . . . do you think I should pass 'Go' and start the game again?

Much love

Jo

WORK BY JO SPENCE

BOOKS

Guidelines Photography, Richard Greenhill, Maggie Murray, Jo Spence; MacDonald, 1978

Reinventing The Family Album: Handbook of Photography for Women, Nina Kellgren, Jo Spence, forthcoming, Camden Press

Photography/Politics: One, Terry Dennett, David Evans, Sylvia Gohl, Jo Spence, Photography Workshop, London 1979

Photography/Politics: Two, Patricia Holland, Jo Spence, Simon Watney, Comedia/Photography Workshop, 1986

ARTICLES

'An Omnibus Dossier', Jo Spence, with Introduction and Afterword by Simon Watney, *Screen*, vol. 24, no. 1, 1983.

'Beyond the Family Album', Jo Spence, *Ten. 8*, no. 4, spring 1980.

'Body Talk' a dialogue between Ros Coward and Jo Spence, *Photography/Politics: Two*, Comedia/Photography Workshop, 1986.

'Body Beautiful, Body in Crisis?' Jo Spence, *Openmind!* June 1986.

'Confronting Cancer', *City Limits*, Jo Spence, 22 July 1983.

'Facing up to Myself', Jo Spence, Annie Brackx, Laura Margolis, *Spare Rib*, no. 68, March 1978.

'Fairy Tales and Photography: Another Look at Cinderella', Jo Spence, unpublished thesis 1981.

'New Portraits for Old', Rosy Martin, Jo Spence, *Feminist Review* 19, Spring 1985.

'Photo Therapy – Transforming the Portrait', Rosy Martin and Jo Spence, *Essays in the Media*, ed. Julienne Dickey, 1987.

'Photography, Ideology and Education', Terry Dennett and Jo Spence, *Screen Education*, no. 21, 1977.

Photography In and Out of Schools, Jackdaw kit, Terry Dennett, Jo Spence, Half Moon Photography Workshop/Photography Workshop, 1978.

'The Picture of Health?', Jo Spence, *Spare Rib*, February and April 1986.

'The Politics of Photography', Jo Spence, *Camerawork*, no. 1, republished in *The British Journal of Photography*, 3 August 1976.

'Public Images, Private Functions', Ed Barber talking to Jo Spence. *Ten. 8*, no. 13, Winter 1983/4.

'Remodelling Photo History – A Collaboration Between Two Photographers', Terry Dennett, Jo Spence, *Screen*, vol. 23, no. 1, 1982.

'Ten Years in Photography Workshop', Terry Dennett, Jo Spence, in *Photographic Practices – Towards a Different Image*, eds S. Bezencenet, P. Corrigan, Comedia 1986.

'The Documentary Forum', a contribution by Jo Spence, *Creative Camera*, February 1986.

'The Sign as a Site of Class Struggle – Reflections on Works by John Heartfield', Jo Spence, *Block V*, 1981, reprinted in *Photography/Politics: Two*, 1986.

'The Unpolitical Photograph?', Terry Dennett, Jo Spence, *Camerawork 7*, 1978.

'What did you do in the war, Mummy?' Jo Spence, *Photography/Politics: One*, Photography Workshop, 1979.

'What do people do all day. Class and gender in images of women', Jo Spence, *Screen Education*, 1980, reprinted in *In Whose Image? Writings on Media Sexism*, eds Kath Davies, Julienne Dickey, The Women's Press 1986.

'What is a political Photograph?', a contribution by Jo Spence, *Camerawork*, 1984.

EXHIBITIONS

Beyond the Family Album, 1979, Jo Spence/Photography Workshop, distributed by Cockpit Gallery, Holborn.

The (British) Workers' Film and Photo League, Terry Dennett, distributed by Photography Workshop, 152 Upper Street, London N1.

Domestic Labour and Visual Representation, Hackney Flashers Collective, slide set from the Society for Education in Film and Television, 29 Old Compton Street, London W.1.

Don't Say Cheese, Say Lesbian, 1987, Rosy Martin and Jo Spence, distributed by Romart Design, 31 Grimthorpe House, Percival Street, London, E.C.1.

Double Exposure, The Minefield of Memory, 1987, Rosy Martin and Jo Spence, distributed by Photographers Gallery.

Family, Fantasy, Photography, 1982, the Polysnappers (Mary Ann Kennedy, Jane Munro, Charlotte Pembrey, Jo Spence), distributed by Cockpit Gallery.

The Home-Made Show, Terry Dennett, distributed by Photography Workshop.

The Photo Therapy Road Show, Rosy Martin and Jo Spence, distributed by Photography Workshop.

The Picture of Health?, Jessica Evans, Rosy Martin, Maggie Murray, Jo Spence, Yana Stajno, two versions, distributed by Photography Workshop.

Review of Work: 1950—1985, Jo Spence, distributed by Photography Workshop.

Strike 26, Terry Dennett, distributed by Photography Workshop.

The Thirties and Today, Terry Dennett, distributed by Photography Workshop.

Who's Holding the Baby? 1979, Hackney Flashers Collective, distributed by Photography Workshop.

The Worker Photographer, agit-prop broadsheet/poster, distributed by Photography Workshop.

PHOTO CREDITS

All photographs are by Jo Spence except for the following:

Michael Balfre *17*
Ed Barber/Jo Spence *79–81*
Clode Family Archive *13, 143*
Terry Dennett *151*
Terry Dennett/Photography Workshop *63*
Terry Dennett/Jo Spence *99, 107, 109, 119, 121–133, 157, 161, 162, 166*
Mark Edwards *83*
Hackney Flashers *69, 70, 73, 75, 76, 77*
Hackney Flashers Archive *67*
Rosy Martin/Jo Spence *11, 111, 149, 170, 176–183, 189, 191, 193, 213, 216*
Rosy Martin/Jo Spence/Maggie Murray *168*
Michael Ann Mullen *108 top*
Maggie Murray (Format)/Jo Spence *163, 164, 165*
Polysnappers *135–141*
David Roberts *173*
David Roberts/Jo Spence *195, 197, 199, 201, 203*
Spare Rib *110*
Stephen Taffler/Photo Coverage *15*

Cover design by Anne Braybon using photos by Rosy Martin/Jo Spence (front cover) and David Roberts (back cover).